NASCAR RACERS

REVISED 2004 EDITION

TODAY'S TOP DRIVERS

BEN WHITE AND NIGEL KINRADE

CRESTLINE

An imprint of MBI Publishing Company

The edition published in 2004 by Crestline, an imprint of MBI
Publishing Company, Galtier Plaza, Suite 200, 380 Jackson Street,
St. Paul, MN 55101-3885 USA

Crestline books are also available at discounts in bulk quantity for
industrial or sales-promotional use. For details, please contact:
Special Sales Manager at MBI Publishing Company, Galtier Plaza,
Suite 200, 380 Jackson Street, St. Paul, MN 55101-3885 USA.

For a free catalog, call 1-800-826-6600, or visit our website at
www.motorbooks.com.

ISBN 0-7603-1981-2

Printed in China

CONTENTS

Acknowledgments 6

Introduction 7

Johnny Benson 9

Greg Biffle 11

Dave Blaney 13

Brett Bodine 17

Jeff Burton 19

Ward Burton 23

Kurt Busch 27

Ricky Craven 31

Dale Earnhardt Jr. 35

Bill Elliott 39

Christian Fittapaldi 43

Jeff Gordon 45

Robby Gordon 49

Kevin Harvick 53

Dale Jarrett 55

Jimmie Johnson 59

Matt Kenseth 63

Bobby Labonte 65

Terry Labonte 69

Sterling Marlin 73

Mark Martin 77

Jeremy Mayfield 81

Jamie McMurray 85

Casey Mears 87

Jerry Nadeau 89

Joe Nemechek 91

Ryan Newman 93

Steve Park 97

Kyle Petty 101

Ricky Rudd 105

Elliott Sadler 109

Jimmy Spencer 111

Tony Stewart 115

Kenny Wallace 119

Rusty Wallace 121

Michael Waltrip 125

Index 128

ACKNOWLEDGMENTS

To my father, the late Ben Newton White Jr. Thank you, Dad, for introducing me to the exciting world of NASCAR Winston Cup racing.

First and foremost, I would like to thank the NASCAR Winston Cup drivers and teams featured in this book for the time they extended to me for this project, as well as past projects in my nearly 20 years of motorsports journalism. Your insight and continued friendship is most appreciated.

A tremendous thanks to Denny Darnell, Rob Goodman, and the entire staff of Sports Marketing Enterprises, R.J. Reynolds Tobacco Co., for helping to provide information both personal and professional concerning each subject featured here. They will be deeply missed, as they have completed their final year as series sponsor after 33 seasons.

Hearty thanks to Nigel Kinrade for his fantastic photographs, all of which are so central to this book. Heather Oakley and Lee Klancher of MBI Publishing Company offered tremendous contributions toward making this book a success.

As always, I'd like to thank Mark Ashenfelter, Kenny Bruce, Rob Fisher, Jon Gunn, Jeff Owens, Steve Waid, Ray Shaw, Whitney Shaw, Kirk Shaw, Art Weinstein, and Deb Williams of NASCAR Winston Cup Illustrated and NASCAR Winston Cup Scene for their continued support.

Finally, a very sincere thank you to my wife, Eva, and son, Aaron. Thank you both for your continued support of a career that has been tremendously rewarding.

—Ben White

Above: Success in NASCAR Winston Cup racing requires a group effort. Just ask 2002 champion Tony Stewart, seen here getting attention from the Joe Gibbs Racing team at North Carolina Speedway in February 2002.
Below: Two NASCAR legends of the future, Jimmie Johnson and Dale Earnhardt Jr., hang loose in the garage area at Pocono Raceway in June 2002.

ew of us get to experience the heart-pounding thrill of pushing a top-of-the-line stock car to its limits around a racetrack. Fewer still possess the elusive combination of skill, courage, and luck that it takes to be a NASCAR winner. As a result, millions of fans around the world look to these favored few as true heroes. So if fate hasn't seen fit to make us Winston Cup champions, then we should at least be able to sit down and chew the fat with our idols of the ovals.

Here we offer an up-close-and-personal look at the leading stock car drivers of our time. Some have faced both glory in the Winner's Circle and near-death encounters on the oval over lengthy, perhaps legendary, careers. Others are so young they barely look old enough to drive. Some come to the sport from veritable racing dynasties with winning pedigrees; others emerged from obscure beginnings and fought mightily just for the chance to prove themselves on the track. The highest of triumphs and lowest of disappointments can be seen in the eyes of these men and women, their actions captured by the photographs within these pages.

Wherever they came from and whatever their background, all the men and women who slide through the window into the driver's seat of a Winston Cup car are motivated by the same force: the unrelenting desire to best a rival in a turn or down a straightaway, and reach the finish line in front of the rest.

Top: Ryan Newman's No. 12 Ford ran at the head of the pack at many events in 2002, helping Newman earn the title of NASCAR Winston Cup Rookie of the Year. The win at New Hampshire International Speedway in September, shown here, was his one victory among many great showings throughout the season.

Above: Under the helmet, all drivers are created equal. Shawna Robinson is the only female driver currently on the NASCAR Winston Cup Circuit, and the first woman to complete a race in more than two decades.

Left: Jubilation! Dale Earnhardt Jr. celebrates a win at Texas Motor Speedway in 2000. The thrill of victory is what it's all about for today's great stock car drivers.

JOHNNY BENSON

10

Born:
June 27, 1963
Grand Rapids, Michigan

Height: 6-0

Weight: 180 lbs

Sponsor	**Valvoline**
Make	**Pontiac**
Crew Chief	**James Ince**
Owner	**MBV Motorsports**

Throughout his seven-year NASCAR Winston Cup career, Johnny Benson, driver of the MBV Motorsports Pontiac, has been close to victory on several occasions. To his disappointment, only one checkered flag has waved over his red, white and blue machine to date. It came on November, 3, 2002 at North Carolina Motor Speedway in Rockingham, N.C. Many times in his past, he had been in position to win, but circumstances beyond his control took him out of the mix in the closing stages.

Benson got accustomed to winning when he won the 1993 American Speed Association championship and continued on in the Busch Series, where he won Rookie of the Year honors in 1994. He followed that by winning the 1995 Busch Series championship. It was clear he could battle fiercely against the sport's biggest names. There was no question he had a bright future ahead of him.

The Michigan native began his Winston Cup career with team owner Chuck Rider in 1996 before moving on to Jack Roush in 1998 and then Tim Beverly in 2000. Nelson Bowers purchased the team 18 races into the 2000 season. It's been a union that has provided some success, but not to the level Benson would like to see.

When asked to describe his 2003 season, Benson replies, "I'd say terrible. That's the one-word answer. It's not what we expected, based on having that win at Rockingham at the end of 2002. We thought we could carry that over. We've had a few small issues to where we just haven't been as good as we would like to see. It's one of those deals."

NASCAR Winston Cup Career Statistics

Year	Races	Wins	Top 5s	Top 10s	Poles	Total Points	Final Standing	Winnings
1996	30	0	1	6	1	3,004	21st	$947,080
1997	32	0	0	8	1	3,575	11th	$1,256,457
1998	32	0	3	10	0	3,160	20th	$1,360,335
1999	34	0	0	2	0	3,012	28th	$1,567,668
2000	33	0	3	7	0	3,716	13th	$1,841,324
2001	36	0	6	14	0	4,152	11th	$2,894,903
2002	31	1	3	7	0	3,132	29th	$2,746,670
2003	36	0	2	4	0	3,448	24th	$3,411,793
Totals	264	1	18	58	2	27,199		$16,026,230

Above: Johnny Benson brings his Pontiac to a stop in the pits at Las Vegas Motor Speedway in March 2002. Left: Benson shows his serious side behind the wheel of his racecar prior to the start of the 2001 Daytona 500.

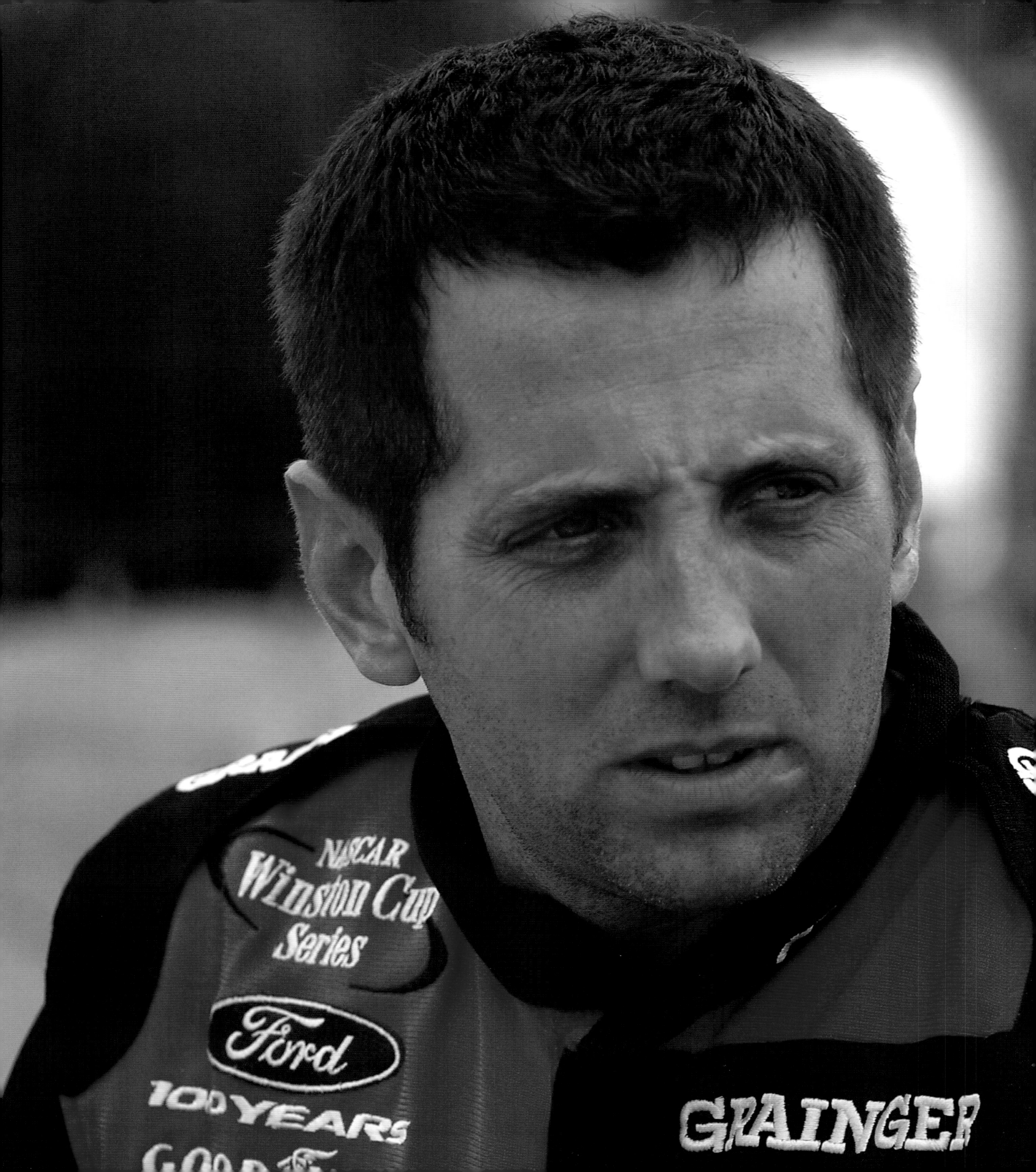

NASCAR
Winston Cup
Series
Ford
100 YEARS
GRAINGER

GREG BIFFLE

16

Born:
December 23, 1969
Vancouver, Washington

Height: 5-9

Weight: 170 lbs

Sponsor	**Grainger**
Make	**Ford**
Crew Chief	**Doug Richert**
Owner	**Jack Rousch**

If one were asked to describe the career of NASCAR Winston Cup driver Greg Biffle, the best definition would be that he's a talented and determined driver who can get the job done. Biffle, a native of Vancouver, Washington, has certainly wasted little time making his presence known around NASCAR circles.

Biffle progressed through the various levels of NASCAR racing before making his NASCAR Winston Cup debut in 2002. But before that huge jump, he logged championships in both the NASCAR Craftsman Truck Series in 2000 and the NASCAR Busch Series in 2002, as well as Rookie of the Year in both divisions. He also ran seven 2002 NASCAR Winston Cup events for team owners Andy Petree, Jack Roush, and Kyle Petty, gaining experience before his 2003 baptism into the most competitive form of auto racing in the world.

Biffle joined NASCAR's elite circuit in 2003 and, by July, scored a victory in the Pepsi 400 at Daytona International Speedway. The win served as a glimpse of good things to come, since a win in one's rookie season shows special talent waiting to be unleashed.

"We've worked harder than we've ever worked, trying to get our race cars where they need to be," Biffle says. "We've struggled some, but it (the win at Daytona) shows how hard these guys work and how they don't give up."

NASCAR Winston Cup Career Statistics

Year	Races	Wins	Top 5s	Top 10s	Poles	Total Points	Final Standing	Winnings
2003	35	1	3	6	0	3,696	20th	$2,410,053
Totals	35	1	3	6	0	3,696	20th	$2,410,053

Opposite Page: Greg Biffle, driver of the No. 16 Roush Racing Ford, seems to be listening to advice in 2003, his rookie season in NASCAR Winston Cup racing. Far Left: Biffle leads Joe Nemechek (25) and Morgan Shepherd (89) during a close battle for position. Left: Biffle enjoys his first career NASCAR Winston Cup victory after conserving fuel in the Pepsi 400 at Daytona International Speedway in July of 2003. Above: On several occasions, Greg Biffle placed his red and black Roush Racing Ford out front, proving his talents in the high-pressured world of NASCAR.

DAVE BLANEY

77

Born:
October 24, 1962
Hartford, Ohio

Height: 5-8

Weight: 170 lbs

Sponsor	Jasper Engines
Make	Dodge
Crew Chief	Robert Barker
Owner	Doug Bawel, Mark Wallace, Mark Harrah

When Dave Blaney first came onto stock car racing's biggest stage for one event in 1992, he was considered a true rookie in the high exposure world of NASCAR Winston Cup racing. His car, which he owned himself, had to carry a yellow rookie stripe on its rear bumper, indicating to the veterans that someone with less experience was racing with them. But he was far from being a rookie—the Hartford, Ohio native had paved the path for that long-awaited start by logging countless laps around race tracks during 10 years of open-wheel competition.

His resume was impressive, much like that of Jeff Gordon, another open-wheel standout who went on to win four NASCAR championships.

In 1984, Blaney had won Rookie of the Year honors on the All-Star Circuit of Champions sprint car series, as well as a USAC Silver Crown championship, becoming the youngest driver to win that division. Then Blaney won the World Sprint Car championship in 1988 at Hagerstown, Maryland. The following season, he posted a remarkable 76 top-five finishes in 85 events in both modified and sprint car events. Further, in 1990, he won the Pacific Coast Nationals at Ascot Speedway in California.

In 1995, he won the Knoxville Nationals, one of the biggest events of open-wheel racing. Also that year, he won the World of Outlaws championship and was named that year's Sprint Car Driver of the Year.

NASCAR Winston Cup Career Statistics

Year	Races	Wins	Top 5s	Top 10s	Poles	Total Points	Final Standing	Winnings
1992	1	0	0	0	0	--	--	$4,500
1999	5	0	0	0	0	--	51st	$212,170
2000	33	0	0	2	0	--	31st	$1,272,689
2001	36	0	0	6	0	--	22nd	$1,827,896
2002	36	0	0	5	0	--	19th	$2,978,593
2003	36	0	0	4	0	3,194	28th	$2,828,692
Totals	147	0	1	17	0	3,194		$9,124,540

Blaney places his yellow and blue Ford at the bottom of the race track in hopes of finding the fastest way around its surface.

Left: Dave Blaney, driver of Jasper Motorsports Ford, enjoys a peaceful moment in the garage area during a break in the action.

Above: Dave Blaney, driver of the Jasper Motorsports Ford, receives service from his crew during a pit stop. Usually, four tires and fuel are added in less than 20 seconds.

Below: Blaney is busy doing what he does best at speed in his familiar yellow and blue Jasper Motorsports machine.

Above: Like so many times during his career, Blaney sits behind the controls of his Jasper Motorsports Ford, prepared to start his engine prior to the start of an event. Right: Blaney stands quietly, possibly anticiapting the quickest line around the race track before attempting a qualifying run.

After two seasons of finishing in the runner-up position in the World of Outlaws sprint car circuit, Blaney was given the opportunity to drive on the NASCAR Busch Series with team owner Bill Davis, winning 1 pole position in 20 starts. By the end of 1999, he had improved in his stock car driving skills to post a seventh-place finish in the NASCAR Busch Series standings, posting 5 top-5s, 12 top-10s, and 4 pole positions in 31 starts.

By 1999, Blaney once again realized the excitement of driving in NASCAR's top division, this time with Davis. His best start that season, a 4th, and best finish, a 23rd, came at Homestead, Florida.

From 2000 through 2002, Blaney improved on his points ranking from 31st 22nd to 19th. But in 2003, mechanical misfortunes and accidents, not of his making, took him out of the top-25 in points.

Still, being one of the top 43 stock car drivers in the world speaks volumes for his over-all ability. As he continues to search for that elusive first NASCAR Winston Cup victory, he involves himself in all facets of racing endeavors, which include owning Sharon Speedway in Hartford, Ohio with his family. He also fields a Sprint Car team for his brother Dale, a former NBA player with the Los Angeles Lakers.

"We've had good runs and some not so good," Blaney says. "This is a great race team and I feel we're making progress toward some real good finishes."

BRETT BODINE

11

Born:
January 11, 1959
Chemung, New York

Height: 5-7

Weight: 160 lbs

Sponsor	**Hooters Restaurants**
Make	**Ford**
Crew Chief	**Buddy Sisco**
Owner	**Brett Bodine**

Since becoming a team owner in NASCAR eight years ago, Brett Bodine has campaigned his own race cars on a budget measured much lower than that of, say, reigning champion Matt Kenseth. You don't need television to see a series featuring a "survivor"—all you have to do is look Brett Bodine's way. Following in his brother Geoffrey's footsteps, Brett first joined NASCAR's elite circuit in 1986.

Brett Bodine had already established himself as a pretty good race car driver when he came on the NASCAR scene, having won track modified championships at various venues across the Northeast. His racing career began in 1977 and worked his way up to the NASCAR Busch Series. In 1986 he came close to winning the series championship, finishing second to Larry Pearson, son of NASCAR legend David Pearson.

In 1998, Bodine was named one of the top 50 modified drivers of all time. He drove for some of the most prominent team owners in the business, including Rick Hendrick, Hoss Ellington, Bud Moore, drag racer–turned–Winston Cup owner Kenny Bernstein, and the legendary driver-turned-owner, Junior Johnson. Bodine's lone victory to date came with Bernstein in 1990 in the First Union 400 at North Wilkesboro.

Bodine bought Johnson's team in 1996, and has served as the team's driver and owner ever since. At times, Bodine has struggled to keep the Winston Cup operation alive, often times thinking of closing the doors of his Mooresville, North Carolina based operation. Still, he continues to hang on in hopes of turning everything around toward becoming a winning race team.

"The one thing that this sport and this life have taught me is that you had better be flexible," Bodine says. "You had better be ready to change, to adapt. You have to be able to survive."

NASCAR Winston Cup Career Statistics

Year	Races	Wins	Top 5s	Top 10s	Poles	Total Points	Final Standing	Winnings
1986	1	0	0	0	0	109	--	$10,100
1987	14	0	0	0	0	1,271	32nd	$51,145
1988	29	0	2	5	0	2,833	20th	$433,658
1989	29	0	1	6	0	3,051	19th	$281,274
1990	29	1	5	9	1	3,440	12th	$442,681
1991	29	0	2	6	1	2,980	19th	$376,220
1992	29	0	2	13	1	3,491	15th	$495,224
1993	29	0	3	9	2	3,183	20th	$582,014
1994	31	0	1	6	0	3,159	19th	$791,444
1995	31	0	0	2	0	2,988	20th	$893,029
1996	30	0	0	1	0	2,814	24th	$767,716
1997	31	0	0	2	0	2,716	29th	$936,694
1998	33	0	0	0	0	2,907	25th	$1,281,673
1999	32	0	0	0	0	2,351	35th	$1,321,396
2000	29	0	0	0	0	2,145	35th	$1,020,659
2001	36	0	0	2	0	2,948	30th	$1,740,526
2002	32	0	0	0	0	2,276	36th	$1,766,820
2003	6	0	0	0	0	308	52nd	$383,718
Totals	480	1	16	61	5	44,970		$13,575,991

Right: Brett Bodine is all set for a competitive run. This time, he's looking for a good finish at Atlanta Motor Speedway in November 2000. Below: Bodine takes the Hooters Ford around the bend at Lowe's Motor Speedway in May 2002.

JEFF BURTON

99

Born:
June 29, 1967
South Boston, Virginia

Height: 5-7

Weight: 155 lbs

Sponsor	**Citgo**
Make	**Ford**
Crew Chief	**Paul Andrews**
Owner	**Jack Roush**

I n 2003, one could honestly say Jeff Burton, driver of the Roush Racing Ford, was in a rebuilding year at Roush Racing. Yes, he has enjoyed an impressive amount of victories in his 10-year Winston Cup career. But like so many of his fellow competitors, he's not going to be satisfied until he reaches the pinnacle of the sport with a Winston Cup championship.

In high school, Burton made a habit of excelling at every sport he entered, following the standard set by his favorite team, the Duke University Blue Devils. As he engaged in some pretty intense go-kart racing, his efforts improved enough to make him a two-time Virginia State champion by the age of seven. By his 17th birthday, Burton was racing the Pure Stock Class at South Boston Speedway, and four years later, he was winning races in double-digits in the track's premier Late Model Stock division.

Burton's first NASCAR win came at Martinsville, Virginia, in the Busch Series in 1990, and he went on to place 15th in points that season. By 1993, the urge to go on to Winston Cup racing was simply too great to ignore. His first start came on July 11th of that year at New Hampshire International Speedway for team owner Filbert Martocci. Burton ran well in the

NASCAR Winston Cup Career Statistics

Year	Races	Wins	Top 5s	Top 10s	Poles	Total Points	Final Standing	Winnings
1993	1	0	0	0	0	52	--	$9,550
1994	30	0	2	3	0	2,726	24th	$594,700
1995	29	0	1	2	0	2,556	32nd	$630,770
1996	30	0	6	12	1	3,538	13th	$884,303
1997	32	3	13	18	0	4,285	4th	$2,296,614
1998	33	2	18	23	0	4,415	5th	$2,626,987
1999	34	6	18	23	0	4,733	5th	$5,725,399
2000	34	4	15	22	1	4,836	3rd	$5,959,439
2001	36	2	8	16	0	4,394	10th	$4,230,737
2002	36	0	5	14	0	4,259	12th	$3,863,220
2003	36	0	3	11	0	4,109	12th	$3,846,884
Totals	331	17	89	144	2	39,873		$30,668,603

Right: Jeff Burton studies information given to him while behind the wheel of his Ford at Phoenix in October 2001. Below: Burton turns his Roush Racing Ford left on the concrete at Las Vegas in March 2002. A strong ninth-place finish there helped put Burton near the top early in the 2002 campaign.

Top: Burton makes a pit stop at Martinsville Speedway. Burton's Roush Racing crew is one of the fastest on the Winston Cup circuit. Middle: Burton races Davey Blaney (No. 93) for position at Dover Downs International Speedway in June 2001. Right: Burton takes aim with champagne in Victory Lane after winning at New Hampshire in July 1998.

opening laps, but fell out after crashing on lap 86 of the 300-lap event.

Over time, Burton attracted attention from several prominent team owners, including Bill and Mickey Stavola, as well as Jack Roush, the organization from which all Burton's wins have come. His best season to date was 1999, when he logged 6 victories, 18 top fives, and 23 top 10s. Burton posted wins that year at Charlotte, both Darlington races, Las Vegas, Rockingham, North Carolina, and the spring race at New Hampshire, where it all began.

Going into the 2004 season, Burton has collected 17 victories since his first start in 1993, but once the team gets back to its winning ways, one can rest assured more wins will be added to his personal win column. Burton is hopeful the points that come with them, coupled with consistency that has been missing in the past, can translate to a championship. To do so, a driver and team must hover around the top three positions all season long.

"We set some goals and our primary goal was to rebuild and reload and use 2003 to get back to the position where we could contend for wins," Burton says. "To use this year to learn and get back to where we need to be. I think we've certainly made progress this year but I also think we've built a better race team and build faster race cars and feel good about all those things."

Right: Burton raises his arms in victory after besting the field at Phoenix International Speedway in November 2000. It was his fourth win of the season, helping Burton achieve his best year to date. Below: Behind the wheel of his Ford, Burton is set to get down to business in this 1998 photograph.

WARD BURTON

22

Born:
October 25, 1961
South Boston, Virginia

Height: 5-6

Weight: 150 lbs

Sponsor	**Caterpillar**
Make	**Dodge**
Crew Chief	**Frankie Stoddard**
Owner	**Bill Davis**

Ward Burton has often been asked why his accent is so different from his younger brother Jeff's. All Ward can do is shrug his shoulders and say, "It's just the way I talk." Ward sounds like a Confederate general—his southern Virginia drawl is as thick and smooth as brown maple syrup. Brother Jeff has it all figured out. When a member of the motorsports media asked Jeff why there was a difference, Jeff replied, "Well, all I can figure is I was born in the northernmost point of the house and Ward was born in the southernmost part."

In the early 1970s, stock car racing came to the Burton family via radio broadcast every Sunday afternoon. Through the excitement of what he heard over the airwaves, Ward chose his all-time sports hero—Winston Cup champion Bobby Alli-

NASCAR Winston Cup Career Statistics

Year	Races	Wins	Top 5s	Top 10s	Poles	Total Points	Final Standing	Winnings
1994	26	0	1	2	1	1,971	35th	$304,700
1995	29	1	3	6	0	2,926	22nd	$634,655
1996	27	0	0	4	1	2,411	33rd	$873,619
1997	31	0	0	7	1	2,987	24th	$1,004,944
1998	33	0	1	5	2	3,352	16th	$1,516,183
1999	34	0	6	16	1	4,062	9th	$2,405,913
2000	34	1	4	17	0	4,152	10th	$2,699,604
2001	36	1	6	10	0	3,846	14th	$3,583,692
2002	36	2	3	8	1	3,362	25th	$4,849,880
2003	36	0	0	4	0	3,550	21st	$3,500,156
Totals	332	5	24	79	7	32,619		$21,374,056

Ward Burton is going full throttle at Las Vegas Motor Speedway in March 2002.

son. Because Allison used No. 12 on most of his cars, Burton claimed the number for his racecars, the go-karts he raced, and even the back of his baseball and football jerseys.

Like his brother Jeff, Ward began racing go-karts at age eight and raced until he was 16 years old. Mini stocks and street stocks appealed to him until late model stocks caught his eye in 1986. By 1989, Burton earned three victories at South Boston, Virginia, as well as most popular driver honors. He finished second in the Rookie of the Year battle in the NASCAR Busch Series in 1990, and he eventually won four races in that division, a forum he continues to enter on occasion.

By 1994, Burton found an open door to the NASCAR Winston Cup circuit through team owner A. G. Dilliard, the father-in-law of driver Rick Mast. The following year, Burton joined Bill Davis, a successful Arkansas businessman who felt a deep passion for the Winston Cup circuit.

Burton capped 1995 with his first career victory, winning at Rockingham late in the season. From there, he scored wins in the prestigious Southern 500 at Darlington Raceway in the spring of 2000 and summer of 2001.

In 2002, Burton stepped his career up to a new plateau by claiming victory at the season-opening Daytona 500, and the New England 300 at Loudon, New Hampshire on July 21.

Since those victories occurred, many changes have taken place among crew members at Bill Davis Racing, including the departure of crew chief Tommy Baldwin. Over the off-season, Davis worked hard to rebuild his team and put them back in victory lane. Those wins simply haven't come.

Late into the 2003 season, Burton spoke to various press members about his

Burton waves to the crowd at pre-race introductions before the start of the Coca-Cola 600 at Charlotte in May 1999.

desire to leave Bill Davis Racing for another race team. In October 2003, he announced he would be joining Gene Haas for the 2004 NASCAR season.

"The thing with us in 2003 has been dealing with what I call the moving chassis," Burton says. "As an example, we won Loudon in 2002 with a good solid chassis set up of springs and shocks and tires. It was something me and Tommy Baldwin, and the guys on the team came up with. That set up now is laps down. We had to change about eight things that would allow me to get the car competitive again and where I could drive it again. So we've definitely struggled with chassis set ups in 2003 and that has dictated our season."

KURT BUSCH

97

Born:
August 4, 1978
Las Vegas, Nevada

Height: 5-11

Weight: 150 lbs

Sponsor	**Rubbermaid**
Make	**Ford**
Crew Chief	**Jimmy Fennig**
Owner	**Jack Roush**

When team owner Jack Roush looks for new talent for his powerhouse Roush Racing NASCAR Winston Cup organization, he does so in a very unique way. He used a "Gong Show" style where drivers are invited to audition for rides in his race cars. The best of the group gets further consideration, while the others must retreat back to the lesser-known divisions where they succeeded and excelled.

That was the case with Kurt Busch, one of Roush's current Winston Cup drivers. His audition, so to speak, came in the fall of 1999 when he was eventually placed in a NASCAR Craftsman Truck Series ride. The next season, Busch logged four victories in that division, which paved the way for a stellar career in the prestigious Winston Cup division.

Busch began racing at age 14 in dwarf cars at Parhump Valley Speedway near Las Vegas and won the division championship in 1995. The next year he won a hobby stock championship, a further step toward becoming a professional racer. Three years passed before he became the youngest driver to win a NASCAR Featherlite Southwest Tour title at age 21. That proved to Roush that Busch could win and prompted the longtime team owner to give Busch a chance to show his talents on the bigger, high-banked tracks.

Busch moved into the NASCAR Winston Cup ranks in 2000, competing in only seven events as not to upset his rookie of the year bid in 2001. He did not win rookie honors and struggled with seven DNFs (Did Not Finish) for the season. The biggest blow of the season was his failure to qualify for the final event of the season, then at Atlanta Motor Speedway. Roush recognized the potential

NASCAR Winston Cup Career Statistics

Year	Races	Wins	Top 5s	Top 10s	Poles	Total Points	Final Standing	Winnings
2000	7	0	0	0	0	613	--	$311,915
2001	35	0	3	6	1	3,081	27th	$2,170,630
2002	36	4	12	20	1	4,641	3rd	$3,723,650
2003	36	4	9	14	0	4,150	11th	$5,020,485
Totals	114	8	24	40	2	12,485		$11,226,680

Right: Kurt Busch is focused and intent as he straps in before the event at Sonoma, California, in June 2002.
Below: Busch's black-and-blue Ford Taurus makes its way around Sonoma's winding road course.

Above: Busch battles with teammate Mark Martin, in the No. 6 Ford, at the 2002 Daytona 500. Team owner Jack Roush switched the two drivers' crews before the season, with impressive results for both. Below: Busch's lightning-fast crew gets the car loaded up and ready to go in pit row at California Speedway in April 2002.

Busch's No. 97 team possessed and elected to make a rather radical move. Roush replaced Busch's entire team with that of fellow Roush driver, Mark Martin, in hopes of giving both teams new life. Veteran crew chief Jimmy Fennig would lead Busch's operation, while Ben Leslie took over the controls of Martin's team.

The switch was perfect. Busch went on to win an incredible four NASCAR Winston Cup races coming at Bristol, Virginia, Martinsville, Virginia, Hampton, Georgia, and Homestead, Florida. Also, he went on to finish third in the Winston Cup point standings with 12 top fives and 20 top '10s and one pole position. Martin's numbers added to one victory, 12 top fives and 22 top 10s with a second-place finish in the point standings behind 2002 champion Tony Stewart.

In the 2003 NASCAR season, Busch's confidence in his abilities to win races and his team's abilities to produce winning race cars couldn't be higher. He won events in convincing fashion at Bristol, California, Michigan and Bristol again. Busch and Co. is thinking championship in 2004 but also know there are other ways to measure the successes of a season.

Above: Busch's Taurus sports a special paint scheme for his victorious run in the final event of the 2002 Winston Cup season, at Homestead, Florida, in November. Below Left: Ready for battle behind a colorful helmet, Busch awaits the command to fire his engine at Dover, Delaware. Below Right: Busch rightly enjoys his first career Winston Cup winner's trophy, earned at Bristol Motor Speedway in March 2002.

RICKY CRAVEN

32

Born:
May 24, 1966
Newburgh, Maine

Height: 5-9

Weight: 165 lbs

Sponsor	**Tide**
Make	**Ford**
Crew Chief	**Scott Miller**
Owner	**Cal Wells**

pot a Winston Cup competitor sporting an orange-and-white uniform and a huge smile on his face, it's a good bet you're looking at Ricky Craven, driver of the PPI Motorsports Ford. Since winning his first Winston Cup race in October 2001, Craven has not been able to hide those pearly whites. Add to that win list a very impressive and popular victory at Darlington, South Carolina in March of 2003 over fellow competitor Kurt Busch. At the conclusion of that event, Craven emerged the winner only after trading paint on several occasions with Busch in the closing laps and being pushed across the start/finish line after the two collided. It is one event that will go down in Darlington history as one of the best in the track's 52-year existence.

The native of Bangor, Maine, likes what he sees these days in a career that has been revitalized with a team owned by Cal Wells. His cars are good. His team is good. Everyone seems to be mentioning Craven's name as the driver to beat in events on the Winston Cup schedule, especially at New Hampshire International Raceway, a track Craven considers his home turf. He has finally found a bit of stability in a personal racing venture that has seen its fair share of turbulence over its 11 years. One needs to look back at Craven's past to truly appreciate his present role with the Wells team.

Craven drove one event for Dick Moroso in 1991, 62 events for owner Larry Hedrick in 1995 and 1996, and then moved over to the prominent Charlotte-based Hendrick Motorsports and team owner Rick Hendrick, for whom he competed in 38 races. A couple of hard crashes with Hendrick's operation in 1996 and Hendrick in 1997 caused some head injuries that heavily influenced Craven's ability behind the controls. After Craven completed only four events in 1998, doctors determined that he was suffering from post-concussion syndrome, a side

NASCAR Winston Cup Career Statistics

Year	Races	Wins	Top 5s	Top 10s	Poles	Total Points	Final Standing	Winnings
1991	1	0	0	0	0	61	--	$3,750
1995	31	0	0	4	0	2,883	24th	$597,054
1996	31	0	3	5	2	3,078	20th	$941,959
1997	30	0	4	7	0	3,108	19th	$1,259,550
1998	11	0	0	1	1	907	46th	$527,875
1999	24	0	0	0	0	1,513	41st	$853,835
2000	16	0	0	0	0	1,175	44th	$636,562
2001	36	1	4	7	1	3,379	21st	$1,996,981
2002	36	0	3	9	2	3,888	15th	$2,493,720
2003	36	1	3	8	0	3,334	27th	$3,116,211
Totals	252	1	17	41	6	23,326		$12,427,497

Ricky Craven puts his PPI Motorsports Ford to the test at North Carolina Speedway at Rockingham in February 2001.

Above: Craven glides along on the low side of Martinsville's near-flat turns in April 2001. Right: Craven displays his first official winner's trophy after his victory at Martinsville in 2001. Below: Looking a bit tired after a long day at Phoenix International Raceway late in the 2001 season, Craven finished well back after being taken out in an accident not of his making.

In October 2001 at Martinsville Speedway, Craven finally collected his first career Winston Cup victory after a long, hard-fought battle with Dale Jarrett.

effect from the terrible spill he took in a multi-car crash at Talladega and a crash during a practice session at Texas. From there, many months of recuperation passed as he tried desperately to keep his driving hopes alive.

Craven managed to run three events late in the 1998 season with Nelson Bowers, and 24 total events for Scott Barbour and Hal Hicks in 1999. Unfortunately, the strong finishes simply didn't come. So when Cal Wells cut driver Scott Sharp from his program and tapped Craven to fill the void, it was the break Craven had been searching for his entire career.

Since joining Wells, he has been victorious twice, once at Martinsville in 2002, but he is quick to say his most memorable win was that famed event at Darlington early in 2003.

"A lot of fans I meet, that finish (at Darlington) is the first thing they mention," Craven says. "I'm really proud that I was a part of something that some people say will go down in the history books, but it's not something I constantly dwell on. In this business, you can't afford to."

Craven admits the Darlington win may someday become a cornerstone of his career.

"I don't think it will really sink in or that I'll reflect on that win until after I'm finished with racing," Craven says. "I think it will be really neat to be able to show the tape of that win to my grand-kids and let them see what their grandpa used to do for a living."

DALE EARNHARDT JR.

8

Born:
October 10, 1974
Kannapolis, North Carolina

Height: 6-0

Weight: 165 lbs

Sponsor	**Budweiser**
Make	**Chevrolet**
Crew Chief	**Tony Eury Jr.**
Owner	**DEI**

I t is true that one must possess a great deal of talent to be considered for one of NASCAR's most prestigious rides. But having the name "Earnhardt" as part of one's signature certainly doesn't hurt.

When the media scouted the new faces coming into the Winston Cup Series in 1999, it came as no surprise to find the name "Dale Earnhardt Jr." on the list of rookies. What did come as a complete surprise to everybody was that a mere two years later, Earnhardt Jr. would be the only Earnhardt on the circuit.

In the wake of the tragic death of his father at Daytona in February 2001, Earnhardt Jr. was looking to carry on the Earnhardt legacy in NASCAR's premier arena—without his famous father at his side offering advice and encouragement. Throughout the rest of that 2001 season, Earnhardt Jr. was a man everyone looked to for strength.

Early photos of Earnhardt Jr. feature him in one of the black-and-gray pit crew uniforms of the RCR Enterprises team his

NASCAR Winston Cup Career Statistics

Year	Races	Wins	Top 5s	Top 10s	Poles	Total Points	Final Standing	Winnings
1999	5	0	0	1	0	500	48th	$162,095
2000	34	2	3	5	2	3,516	16th	$2,801,880
2001	36	3	9	15	2	4,460	8th	$5,827,542
2002	36	2	11	16	2	4,270	11th	$4,570,980
2003	36	2	13	21	0	4,815	3rd	$4,923,497
Totals	147	9	36	58	6	17,561		$18,285,995

Right: Dale Earnhardt Jr. enjoys an unexpected beer shower in Victory Lane at Richmond, Virginia, in May 2000. It was his second win that season. Below: The red-and-white No. 8 Chevy has come to symbolize Dale Earnhardt Jr. as much as the black-and-silver No. 3 was made famous by his father, the late Dale Earnhardt Sr.

father drove for. Long before he was old enough to possess a North Carolina driver's license, Earnhardt Jr. had his sights set on becoming a racecar driver just like his dad. He was so serious about this venture that he and his brother Kerry pulled an old 1978 Chevrolet Monte Carlo from the woods and welded roll bars within its stripped interior. Worried that the car wouldn't be safe, their father decided to help his young sons and began offering racing advice. Still, he wanted them to work on their own cars to learn the mechanical side of what makes them go fast.

After a few years campaigning on the short tracks around his Mooresville, North Carolina, home, Earnhardt Jr. was ready to try his hand on the super-speedways. He earned a Busch Series ride with Dale Earnhardt Inc. in 1996. He started that first event at Myrtle Beach in 7th position and finished 14th. The powerhouse started by his late father and stepmother Teresa in 1995 came to be a racing home for Earnhardt Jr. He rewarded them with back-to-back Busch Series championships, in his first year and again in 1999.

The inevitable rise to what was known as the Winston Cup circuit came in 1999, when he drove five events. The following year he competed for Rookie of the Year honors, but fell shy to Matt Kenseth by a mere 42 points. When Earnhardt Jr. won his first career Busch Series race in his 16th start, his father was there to celebrate in Victory Lane. And when he won his first Winston Cup race in April of 2000, his father was there, too, as a competitor. The victory celebration was one to remember. Earnhardt Jr. paid homage to his father one more time by winning "The Winston" special non-points event for drivers who had won races during the previous season.

Left: With his car low and at full speed, Earnhardt Jr. does what he does best: racing in Winston Cup competition. Below: In a very short period of time, Dale Jr. established himself as a winning driver. He claimed his second straight NASCAR Busch Series title at the close of the 1999 season.

In 2001, Earnhardt Jr. achieved three emotional victories. First was the win at Daytona in July, the place of his father's death just a few months earlier. The second win came at Dover in the first NASCAR event after the September 11 terrorist attacks on New York City and Washington. The third came at Talladega, Alabama, the sight of his father's final career victory.

Many people consider Dale Earnhardt Jr. to be a viable candidate for winning a Winston Cup championship. His first three full seasons saw him finish 16th, 8th, and 11th in the point standings. In 2003, he remained in the top five in points for the majority of the season.

Even if he doesn't win a championship, he is still quite happy with himself and what he has already accomplished in his short but prosperous racing career.

"It's not important to me to have X amount of accomplishments or have so many things in the pages of NASCAR history attributed to me," Earnhardt Jr. said in NASCAR Illustrated. "I would like to be considered a good race car driver, maybe one of the better race car drivers of the past decade. I think I need more time to get the foot down there. I think it's possible that I can win some championships, but that's not as important to me as maintaining."

BILL ELLIOTT

9

Born:
October 8, 1955
Dawsonville, Georgia

Height: 6-1

Weight: 185 lbs

Sponsor	**Dodge Dealers**
Make	**Dodge**
Crew Chief	**Mike Ford**
Owner	**Ray Evernham**

Former Winston Cup champion Bill Elliott is enjoying one last resurgence in his 26-year NASCAR career before eventually retiring to the north Georgia mountains where he was raised. A victory late in the 2001 season at Homestead, Florida—the 41st win of his career—ended a six-year winless streak. When the checkered flag fell over his Ray Evernham–owned Dodge, it silenced the critics who claimed that Elliott was simply too old to find Victory Lane again.

Elliott wasn't finished. In 2002, he won pole position at Pocono, Pennsylvania and Loudon, New Hampshire in back to back efforts and continued that good fortune with a win at Pocono and the prestigious Brickyard 400 at Indianapolis Motor Speedway the next week.

Stock car racing has been all the redhead from Georgia has ever known. He and his brothers Ernie and Dan got started early, scrounging around their father's junkyard and fixing up old cars that were perfect for racing—around the dirt roads between junk piles, that is. The boys of George and Mildred Elliott had found their calling.

With George acting as an early sponsor and financier, the fledgling race team spent summer weekends competing on small dirt tracks. The brothers eventually persuaded their father to buy a Winston Cup machine, a beat-up old Ford Torino purchased from Bobby Allison. The boys first raced the car at Rockingham, North Carolina, on February 29, 1976, with Bill finishing 33rd in his Winston Cup debut. Still, the boys felt rich with the $640 in prize money they collected.

They struggled mightily for the next few years and threatened more than once to close the doors on the team for good. Thankfully, businessman Harry Melling entered the picture, provided the Elliotts with top-notch equipment, and the wins began to come.

The first victory finally came in the last

NASCAR Winston Cup Career Statistics

Year	Races	Wins	Top 5s	Top 10s	Poles	Total Points	Final Standing	Winnings
1976	7	0	0	0	0	556	49th	$11,635
1977	10	0	0	2	0	1,002	36th	$20,575
1978	10	0	0	5	0	1,176	34th	$42,065
1979	14	0	1	5	0	1,709	28th	$57,450
1980	11	0	0	4	0	1,232	35th	$42,545
1981	13	0	1	7	1	1,442	31st	$70,320
1982	21	0	8	9	1	2,718	25th	$226,780
1983	30	1	12	22	0	4,279	3rd	$479,965
1984	30	3	13	24	4	4,377	3rd	$660,226
1985	28	11	16	18	11	4,191	2nd	$2,433,187
1986	29	2	8	16	4	3,844	4th	$1,069,142
1987	29	6	16	20	8	4,202	2nd	$1,619,210
1988	29	6	15	22	6	4,488	1st	$1,574,639
1989	29	3	8	14	2	3,774	6th	$854,570
1990	29	1	12	16	2	3,999	4th	$1,090,730
1991	29	1	6	12	2	3,535	11th	$705,605
1992	29	5	14	17	2	4,068	2nd	$1,692,381
1993	30	0	6	15	2	3,774	8th	$955,859
1994	31	1	6	12	1	3,617	10th	$936,779
1995	31	0	4	11	2	3,746	8th	$996,816
1996	24	0	0	6	0	2,627	30th	$716,506
1997	32	0	5	14	1	3,836	8th	$1,607,827
1998	32	0	0	5	0	3,305	18th	$1,618,421
1999	34	0	1	2	0	3,246	21st	$1,624,101
2000	32	0	3	7	0	3,267	21st	$2,580,823
2001	36	1	5	9	2	3,824	15th	$3,618,017
2002	36	2	6	13	4	4,158	13th	$3,753,490
2003	36	1	9	12	0	4,303	9th	$4,321,185
Totals	731	44	175	319	55	90,295		$35,380,849

Bill Elliott's red Ray Evernham Dodges proudly carry the number 9. Elliott first made that number famous in Fords owned by the late Harry Melling in the mid-1980s.

race of the 1983 season at Riverside, California, young Elliott's 117th career start. He posted three more wins in 1984 to set the stage for an incredible 1985 season. Bill won 11 races in 28 starts, starting his assault by dominating the Daytona 500. He won at Atlanta and Darlington, and overwhelmed the competition at Talladega in May, winning the pole position with a speed of 202.398 miles per hour. He broke an oil line during the race, but made up 5 miles under green conditions by turning lap after lap at more than 205 miles per hour, regaining the lost deficit to win the race.

The come-from-behind victory at Talladega was his second win of the four major NASCAR events. To win three meant he would be awarded a $1 million bonus from series spon-

sor R.J. Reynolds. Elliott suffered brake problems at the next $1 million eligible event at Charlotte, but came back at Darlington to win the Southern 500 and the bonus in its inaugural year.

In August 1987, Elliott turned the fastest time in a stock car, reaching 212.809 miles per hour at Talladega. He was crowned (then) Winston Cup champion in 1988. From 1995 to 2000, Elliott again fielded his own cars

Top: During the years he held the roles of both driver and team owner, the Georgia native has worn many hats. Left: Elliott likes the response he hears when introduced to the fans at Charlotte in May 2001. His career has enjoyed a nice resurgence in his later years. Right: With his son Chase, Elliott smiles for the cameras after the elder Elliott won one of two 125-mile qualifying events prior to the 2000 Daytona 500.

with co-owner Charles Hardy, but the two never could break into the Winner's Circle. When Elliott joined Evernham at the start of the 2001 season, veteran motorsports writers were predicting them to win multiple races and billed them as a dream team of sorts. The strings of multi-wins haven't come, but Elliott did prove that he could still win races.

Elliott feels his career has been a good one. But toward the end of the 2003 season, he strongly contemplated retiring from the sport. He may choose a very limited schedule in 2004.

"I'm at the age that don't many people go very much past," Elliott says. "As hard as the competition is today and the level of competition, I think that's going to be a factor. I do know I'm on the shorter end of the stick, whether it's this year, next year, or the year after."

Top Left: Elliott signs an autograph for one of his many fans. Elliott has been named the National Motorsports Press Association Driver of the Year on 13 occasions. **Top Right:** Elliott poses for the cameras at Rockingham, North Carolina, in the early months of the 1997 Winston Cup season. That year, Elliott drove his own Fords that were housed in Dawsonville, Georgia. **Bottom Left:** Elliott's Dodge is one of the most recognizable racecars on the track. Here, he is pushing the throttle at Atlanta in March 2002.

CHRISTIAN FITTAPALDI

44

Born:
January 18, 1971
Sao Paulo, Brazil

Height: 5-10

Weight: 160 lbs

Sponsor	**Cheerios**
Make	**Dodge**
Crew Chief	**Gary Putnam**
Owner	**Petty Enterprises**

NASCAR Winston Cup Career Statistics

Year	Races	Wins	Top 5s	Top 10s	Poles	Total Points	Final Standing	Winnings
2003	15	0	0	0	0	857	44th	$1,265,835
Totals	15	0	0	0	0	857		$1,265,835

If one driver could bring an international flavor to NASCAR Winston Cup Series racing, it would be Christian Fittapaldi. He is the nephew of open-wheel legend Emerson Fittapaldi, a two-time winner of the Indianapolis 500 and former CART and Formula One champion.

With his thick Brazilian accent, Fittapaldi would readily admit 2003 was a season of learning about the 3,700-pound stock cars which are so intricate that they often challenge veterans.

Fittapaldi, a native of Sao Paulo, Brazil, began racing go-karts at age 11 in 1982. In the early 1990s, he began racing the larger open-cockpit machines and spent eight seasons in the CART Series driving for actor/team owner Paul Newman and co-owner Carl Haas. During his open-wheel career, he posted two victories, in 1999 at Road America and in 2000 at California Speedway. Before his venture with Newman, Fittapaldi had competed in Formula One competition from 1992 through 1994 with limited success.

In 2001, Kyle Petty, a longtime competitor in NASCAR Winston Cup competition and chief executive officer of Petty Enterprises, offered Fittapaldi a chance to try his hand at stock car racing. His first start came in the final NASCAR Busch Series event that season at Homestead, Florida where he finished 39th.

Fittapaldi made his Winston Cup debut in November of 2002 in Phoenix, Arizona where a crash left him 41st in the final finishing order. That same year, he entered two NASCAR Busch Series events with only mediocre success.

In 2003, his best finish came with a 24th place finish at Pocono, Pennsylvania on July 27th.

His brief NASCAR Winston Cup career has definitely been one of intense study.

Fortunately, he is with the team that has the most victories and most championships in NASCAR's 54 year history.

"Richard (Petty) and Kyle have really changed my life around. It's almost upside down now, but to be with an organization like Petty Enterprises is a tremendous opportunity," Fittapaldi says. "There is a lot of tradition and history at Petty Enterprises, and to be a part of this team is pretty special. The guys on his crew work really hard. Myself and Gary (Putnam, crew chief) have worked a lot to get familiar with each other. The more time we have together the more the chemistry will come together for the Cheerios team."

Opposite Page: Christain Fittipaldi, driver of the Petty Enterprises Dodge, spends a quiet moment as he anticipates an upcoming event. Above: Fittapaldi wheels the famed car No. 43 that was made so famous over the years by its owner, seven-time champion, Richard Petty.

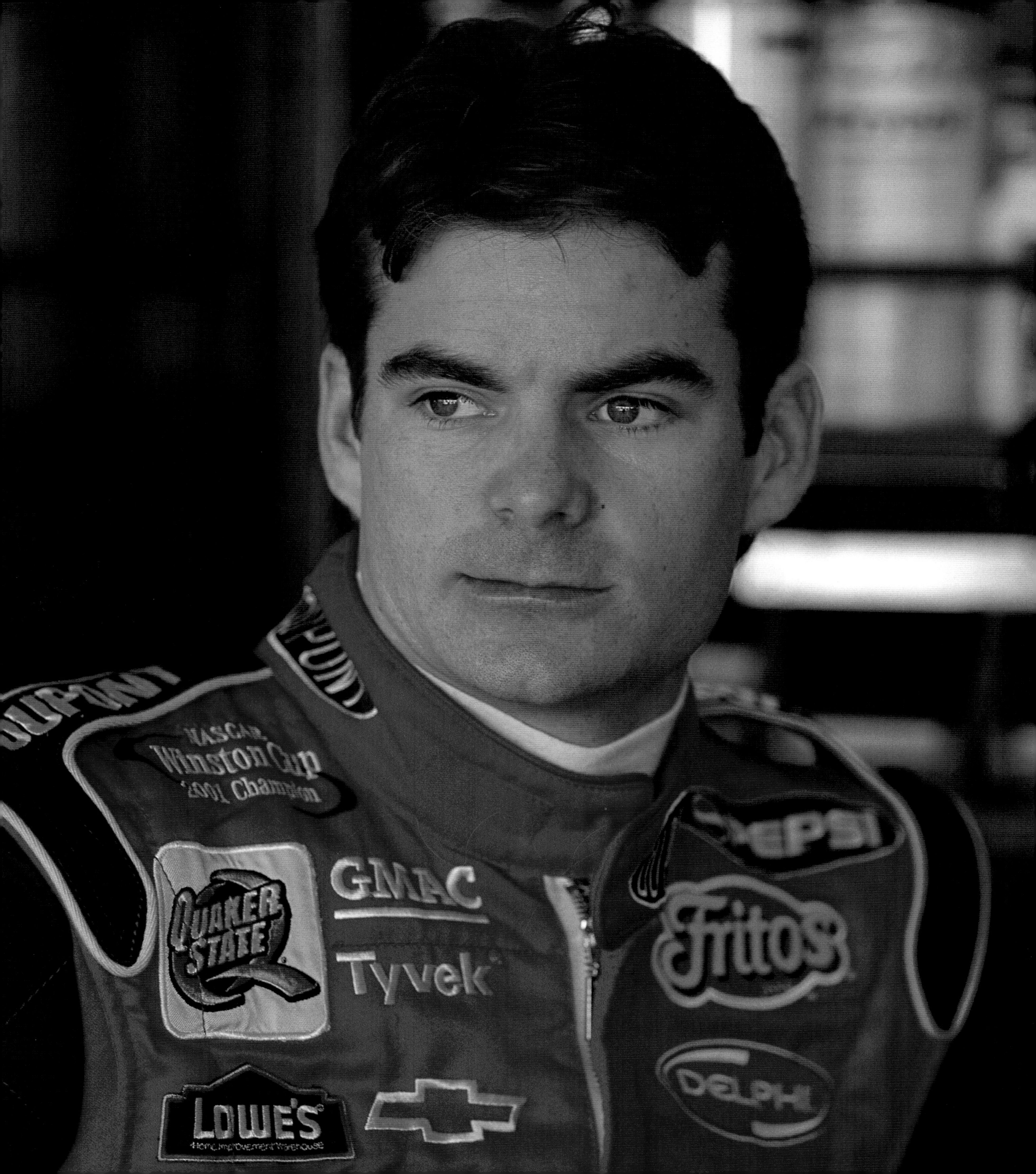
NASCAR
Winston Cup
2001 Champion
QUAKER STATE
GMAC
Tyvek
Fritos
DELPHI
LOWE'S

JEFF GORDON

24

Born:
August 4, 1971
Vallejo, California

Height: 5-7

Weight: 150 lbs

Sponsor	**DuPont**
Make	**Chevrolet**
Crew Chief	**Robbie Loomis**
Owner	**Rick Hendrick**

Not since "The King" Richard Petty first showed up on the NASCAR grids in 1958 has such a young driver shown, and gone on to fulfill, such overwhelming promise as Jeff Gordon. By the time he was 30 years old, Gordon had four Winston Cup titles under his belt— only the third driver ever to win that many—and he is widely considered the man most likely to break Petty's record of seven championships. With his good looks and astounding success, Gordon has established himself as a household name to both veteran fans and schoolchildren.

Gordon's talent showed itself early. The Vallejo, California, native began his racing career at age five in quarter midgets and go-karts. Over the next 15 years, awards and records fell to Gordon like dominos in every mode of open-wheel short-track racing.

When he was still a teenager, Gordon garnered offers from prestigious teams in several forms of auto racing, including one from former Formula One world champion Jackie Stewart. In the end, Gordon chose stock cars.

He attended the Buck Baker Driving School in early 1990 and simply loved the experience. With pillows stuffed inside a seat clearly too big for him, Gordon quickly got a handle on the heavier, bulkier stock cars and was turning some impressive times by the end of the day.

In his first year in the Busch Series division, Gordon won 1991 Rookie of the Year honors driving for owner Bill Davis. In 1992, he won 11 Busch Series pole positions and scored 3 victories. When he was

NASCAR Winston Cup Career Statistics

Year	Races	Wins	Top 5s	Top 10s	Poles	Total Points	Final Standing	Winnings
1992	1	0	0	0	0	70	--	$6,285
1993	30	0	7	11	1	3,447	14th	$765,168
1994	31	2	7	14	1	3,776	8th	$1,779,523
1995	31	7	17	23	8	4,614	1st	$4,347,343
1996	31	10	21	24	5	4,620	2nd	$3,428,485
1997	32	10	22	23	1	4,710	1st	$6,375,658
1998	33	13	26	28	7	5,328	1st	$9,306,584
1999	34	7	18	21	7	4,620	6th	$5,858,633
2000	34	3	11	22	3	4,361	9th	$3,001,144
2001	36	6	18	24	6	5,112	1st	$10,879,757
2002	36	3	13	20	3	4,607	4th	$4,981,170
2003	36	3	15	20	4	4,785	4th	$5,107,762
Totals	365	64	175	230	46	50,050		$55,837,512

Jeff Gordon takes to the treacherous 1.366-mile Darlington Raceway. On this occasion in March 2002, he finished a disappointing ninth, but Gordon has been victorious on five occasions at the track since 1992.

Top: A popular target for the media, Gordon takes a moment to speak to photographers at Daytona in 1998. Above: Gordon makes a scheduled pit stop for tires and fuel while racing his Hendrick Motorsports Chevrolet at Martinsville in 2001.

ready to make his Winston Cup debut at the final event of the 1992 season at Atlanta, he had to get written permission from his parents, since he was not yet 21 years old. He finished unremarkably, in 31st place, but his career soon took off after being signed to a Winston Cup contract by owner Rick Hendrick for the 1993 season.

Gordon established himself in the NASCAR Winston Cup ranks in immediate fashion. He was named Rookie of the Year in 1993 and earned the distinction of becoming the youngest driver to win a 125-mile qualifying race at Daytona International Speedway.

Gordon started his 1994 season by winning the Busch Clash, a special non-points event. He grabbed his first Winston Cup win at the Coca-Cola 600 at Charlotte Motor Speedway in May, and followed that with a victory in the Brickyard 400 at Indianapolis Motor Speedway in August,

making him the first stock car driver to grace Indy's coveted victory circle.

In 1995, only his third full season, Gordon accomplished the unthinkable by winning the Winston Cup championship over the likes of Dale Earnhardt, Terry Labonte, and Rusty Wallace. He was the youngest Winston Cup champion in the modern era (since 1972) and the second youngest ever (1950 NASCAR champion Bill Rexford was only a few months younger). Gordon went on to collect further Winston Cup championships in 1997, 1998, and 2001 to become the winningest active driver.

Over the past couple of seasons, Gordon has struggled to get back to championship form. If mechanical problems didn't haunt him, it was constantly being caught up in someone else's misfortune on the race track. He often looks back on 2001 as one of the defining moments of his career.

Left: In August 1998, Gordon celebrated his second career victory in the prestigious Brickyard 400 at Indianapolis Motor Speedway. Top Right: Hidden behind his familiar multicolored helmet, Gordon gathers his thoughts before race time. Bottom Right: Looking more like someone who should be flipping burgers at the local drive-through than a man at the top of his sport, a young Gordon gleefully accepts his first championship trophy in November 1995. It was the first of four—and counting.

ROBBY GORDON

31

Born:
January 2, 1969
Cerriots, California

Height: 5-10

Weight: 180 lbs

Sponsor	**Cingular**
Make	**Chevrolet**
Crew Chief	**Kevin Hamilton**
Owner	**Richard Childress**

Like so many who began their careers in motorsports other than stock car racing, Robby Gordon didn't grow up driving Chevrolets, Dodges, or Fords, but off-road championship machines beginning in 1985.

Gordon wasted little time making a name for himself. He became the overall winner of the Baja 1000 in 1987 and 1989 and also won the Mickey Thompson Stadium Series championships in 1988 and 1989.

In 1991, Gordon began racing in the IMSA road race series for longtime NASCAR Winston Cup team owner Jack Roush. Gordon became a four-time winner of the 24 Hours of Daytona in the IMSA GTS class in four consecutive years, all for Roush Racing. That led to the open-wheel Indy Car machines for his first full season in 1993, driving for the legendary A. J. Foyt.

NASCAR Winston Cup Career Statistics

Year	Races	Wins	Top 5s	Top 10s	Poles	Total Points	Final Standing	Winnings
1991	2	0	0	0	0	--	55th	$27,265
1993	1	0	0	0	0	--	94th	$17,665
1994	1	0	0	0	0	--	76th	$7,965
1996	3	0	0	0	1	--	57th	$32,915
1997	20	0	1	1	0	--	40th	$622,439
1998	1	0	0	0	0	--	67th	$24,765
2000	17	0	1	2	0	--	43rd	$620,781
2001	17	1	2	3	0	--	44th	$1,371,900
2002	36	0	1	5	0	--	20th	$917,020
2003	36	2	4	10	0	3,856	16th	$3,705,320
Totals	134	3	9	21	1	3,856		$7,348,035

Opposite Page: Robbie Gordon, driver of the No. 31 RCR Enterprises Chevrolet, leans on the rear spoiler of his Chevy during a break in the action at Watkins Glen, N.Y. in August of 2003. Gordon later used his road course racing skills to win the event in convincing fashion. Below: Gordon pushes the No. 31 RCR Enterprises Chevrolet toward the front on of one NASCAR's many high-banked superspeedways.

Above: Gordon raises his hand in celebration as the winner as he stands in victory lane at Watkins Glen. Left: Robbie Gordon, driver of the No. 31 RCR Enterprises Chevrolet, gets left side tires and fuel before returning to action.

Beginning in the early 1990s, Gordon was also busy wheeling NASCAR machines on limited schedules for such legendary team owners as Junie Donlavey, Robert Yates, Felix Sabates, and even the late Dale Earnhardt, to name a few.

By 1996, the bug returned for more off-road racing, and he logged four wins and the SCORE Off-Road Trophy Truck Championship.

Gordon survived one of his most frightening accidents in the 1997 Indianapolis 500 after qualifying 12th. On the 19th lap, fire broke out in the cockpit of his car and he suffered second and third degree burns to his hands, wrist, and right thigh. The injuries sidelined him for a month. He came back for two more seasons, one of which was with a team he owned himself, before directing his attention to NASCAR Winston Cup racing.

In November of 2001, Gordon logged his first career victory at Loudon, New Hampshire while driving in 10 events for team owner Richard Childress. He joined Childress fulltime in 2002 and was winless that first full season, but scored victories on the road courses at Sonoma, California and Watkins Glen, New York in 2003.

Gordon feels he is finally with the right team, one than can provide the stellar equipment he needs to win races.

"We go to the wind tunnel every week and we continue to develop our racing program to me more competitive," Gordon says. "I think the key is running hard every weekend. (NASCAR) racing is so competitive and you can't make any mistakes."

Gordon raises his arms in triumph after a stellar winning performance at Watkins Glen, N.Y. in August of 2003.

KEVIN HARVICK

29

Born:
December 8, 1975
Bakersfield, California

Height: 5-10

Weight: 175 lbs

Sponsor	**GM Goodwrench**
Make	**Chevrolet**
Crew Chief	**Gil Martin**
Owner	**Richard Childress**

These days, the name Kevin Harvick is a common household name in NASCAR Winston Cup racing. But that wasn't the case until the tragic, untimely death of the late Dale Earnhardt in 2001.

Only a Hollywood screenwriter could have dreamed up Kevin Harvick's seemingly unbelievable debut in Winston Cup racing that year. When the season began, Harvick was just a second-year Busch Series driver for Richard Childress, a year removed from being named Busch.

Series Rookie of the Year in 2000; by the end of 2001, Harvick had two Winston Cup victories, the Winston Cup 2001 Rookie of the Year, and the Busch Series championship under his seatbelt.

Harvick's rise was so surprising because no one could have foreseen the fate of Childress' top driver, legendary seven-time champion Earnhardt. After the black day of February 18, 2001, when Earnhardt was killed on the final lap of the Daytona 500, Childress turned to his new young talent to wheel his Winston Cup cars.

Harvick was quick to make an impact. He scored a photo-finish victory over Jeff Gordon in his third career start, coming at Atlanta only two weeks after Earnhardt's death. Despite the hectic, cross-country schedule, Harvick campaigned in both what was then the Winston Cup and Busch Series divisions simultaneously. The effort paid off. Harvick not only went on to notch a second big-league triumph, at the inaugural Winston Cup event at Chicago, but he also posted several Busch Series races en route to that division's 2001 championship. Counting a NASCAR Craftsman Truck Series event, Harvick entered 70 races in three different series during his remarkable year.

The biggest victory of his career came in the 2003 Brickyard 400 at Indianapolis

NASCAR Winston Cup Career Statistics

Year	Races	Wins	Top 5s	Top 10s	Poles	Total Points	Final Standing	Winnings
2001	35	2	6	16	0	4,406	9th	$4,302,202
2002	35	1	5	8	1	3,501	21st	$3,748,100
2003	36	1	11	18	1	4,770	5th	$4,994,249
Totals	106	4	22	42	2	12,677		$13,044,551

Motor Speedway. It was just another example of his continued growth as a competitor that may someday translate into joining that list of NASCAR champions. All told, the Bakersfield, California native has four career NASCAR Winston Cup wins to his credit.

Harvick credits his team owner, Richard Childress, for helping him adjust to the high pressure world of NASCAR Winston Cup racing.

"Last year, I learned a lot, and Richard taught me how to get through a lot of situations," Harvick says. "Richard has a good way of talking to all of us to make it all positive, it's going to be Ok. He's been here and done that several times."

"...I think this season's paid dividends in a lot of different ways."

Bottom Left: After filling the spot of Dale Earnhardt's No. 3 Chevy for RCR Enterprises, Kevin Harvick's No. 29 Chevy has become well known on the Winston Cup circuit. Above: To the surprise of the racing world, Harvick collected his first Winston Cup win in only the third race of his career, at Atlanta in 2001.

DALE JARRETT

88

Born:
November 26, 1956
Conover, North Carolina

Height: 6-2

Weight: 215 lbs

Sponsor	**UPS**
Make	**Ford**
Crew Chief	**Brad Parrott**
Owner	**Robert Yates**

ale Jarrett, driver of the No. 88 Robert Yates Racing Ford, learned early in his driving career that some seasons simply aren't going to go as well as others. He doesn't have to look far to find that season. The 2003 season was certainly not his best.

It was his famous father, Ned Jarrett, a two-time NASCAR Grand National champion in his own right, who taught him the journey could be long and hard and unpredictable.

The younger Jarrett wasted little time experiencing that for himself. He started racing in 1977 at Hickory Motor Speedway in the Limited Sportsman Division before jumping over to the Busch Series when it started in 1982. He launched his Winston Cup career in 1984 during a one-race ride with former driver and team owner Emmanuel Zervackis at Martinsville, Virginia. He started 24th, finished 14th, and collected $1,515 for his first Winston Cup start.

A variety of team owners called on Jarrett to wheel their cars before Cale Yarborough included him in his retirement plans of 1989. Jarrett was to split the schedule with the three-time Winston Cup champion. At the conclusion of that season, however, Yarborough brought in a new driver, and Jarrett found himself without a ride. Fortunately, the search for a new team didn't last long.

When Neil Bonnett, driver of the Wood Brothers Ford, was injured in a crash at Darlington in 1990, Jarrett was tapped to fill the void, presumably for just a race or two. Bonnett's injuries required a lengthy recovery period, however, and Jarrett was put in the driver's seat for the duration of the season.

In August of 1991, Jarrett captured his first career Winston Cup win after battling head-to-head with Davey Allison at Michigan

NASCAR Winston Cup Career Statistics

Year	Races	Wins	Top 5s	Top 10s	Poles	Total Points	Final Standing	Winnings
1984	3	0	0	0	0	267	--	$7,345
1986	1	0	0	0	0	76	--	$990
1987	24	0	0	2	0	2,177	25th	$143,405
1988	29	0	0	1	0	2,622	23rd	$118,640
1989	29	0	2	5	0	2,789	24th	$232,317
1990	24	0	1	7	0	2,558	25th	$214,495
1991	29	1	3	8	0	3,124	17th	$444,256
1992	29	0	2	8	0	3,251	19th	$418,648
1993	30	1	13	18	0	4,000	4th	$1,242,394
1994	30	1	4	9	0	3,298	16th	$881,754
1995	31	1	9	14	1	3,584	13th	$1,363,158
1996	31	4	17	21	2	4,568	3rd	$2,985,418
1997	32	7	20	23	3	4,696	2nd	$3,240,542
1998	33	3	19	22	2	4,619	3rd	$4,019,657
1999	34	4	24	29	0	5,262	1st	$6,649,596
2000	34	2	15	24	3	4,684	4th	$5,984,475
2001	36	4	12	19	4	4,612	5th	$5,366,242
2002	36	2	10	18	1	4,415	9th	$3,935,670
2003	36	1	1	7	0	3,358	26th	$4,055,487
Totals	531	31	152	235	16	64,040		$41,304,489

Driving for Robert Yates Racing, Dale Jarrett puts his UPS-sponsored Ford through the paces at Darlington Raceway in March 2002. A victory at Pocono in June was his first of the season.

International Speedway, beating the late Alabama driver to the finish line by a foot.

The next year, Jarrett left Wood Brothers to join the untested Joe Gibbs organization, a move that sparked much criticism. Jarrett brought the team to prominence with a victory over Dale Earnhardt in the 1993 Daytona 500.

Jarrett was again called upon to fill in after Ernie Irvan was gravely injured in an accident during a practice session at Michigan International Speedway in August 1994. Jarrett was released from his contract with Gibbs and took over Irvan's place with the Robert Yates team for the 1995 season.

Despite questions about whether he was experienced enough to take on such a potent ride, Jarrett quickly silenced the critics, winning at Pocono in July and finishing in the top 10 in 14 of 31 races that year. When Irvan miraculously returned for the full season in 1996, Jarrett moved to a second Yates Ford team with crew chief Todd Parrott at the helm. The results were nothing short of dominant.

In 1996, Jarrett won the Daytona 500, the Coca-Cola 600 at Charlotte, the Brickyard 400 at Indianapolis, and the Miller 400 at Brooklyn, Michigan. After a season-long bid for the Winston Cup championship, Jarrett finished a close third behind Terry Labonte and Jeff Gordon.

Three years later, Jarrett finally added that elusive jewel to his crown by claiming the 1999 NASCAR Winston Cup championship with Robert Yates Racing.

Jarrett won at Rockingham, North Carolina in February of 2003, but since that trip to victory lane, very few positives have come to the Conover, North Carolina native. He's been around the sport long enough to know winners go through slumps from time to time and eventually return to prominence.

"Most teams go through this type of cycle, where things go from good to bad," Jarrett says in NASCAR Illustrated. "The problem is, you can't allow yourself to get into a hole and not pay attention to what's going on around you. All of a sudden, the whole world has changed in the garage area.

"If you look back over the history of the sport, you'll find that pretty much every race team that has been successful has been through situations like this. Maybe most of them didn't fall as far down as we have this year or hit bottom as hard, but they have all been through it."

Top: Late in the 2001 season, Jarrett catches a quiet moment in the garage area of Kansas Speedway. Bottom Left: Jarrett calls upon his crew for tires and fuel at Darlington Raceway in September 2000. Bottom Right: Jarrett discusses the performance of the racecar with crew chief Todd Parrott at Daytona in July 1999. Jarrett left Daytona that weekend as the race winner, furthering him on the way to a Winston Cup championship.

Above: Jarrett is all smiles at Pocono Raceway in this photo taken in July 2000. Right: In August of 1999, Jarrett earned one of his most prestigious victories in the Brickyard 400 at Indianapolis Motor Speedway. Below: Jarrett enjoys the moment after collecting his second career Daytona 500 trophy in February 2000. His first Daytona 500 win came in 1993.

JIMMIE JOHNSON

48

Born:
September 17, 1975
El Cajon, California

Height: 5-11

Weight: 175 lbs

Sponsor	Lowe's Home Improvement
Make	Chevrolet
Crew Chief	Chad Knaus
Owner	Rick Hendrick

NASCAR Winston Cup Career Statistics

Year	Races	Wins	Top 5s	Top 10s	Poles	Total Points	Final Standing	Winnings
2001	3	0	0	0	0	210	--	$122,320
2002	36	3	6	21	5	4,600	5th	$2,847,700
2003	36	3	14	20	2	4,932	2nd	$5,517,850
Totals	75	6	20	41	7	9,742		$8,487,870

At the start of the 2002 NASCAR Winston Cup season, new associations were formed between drivers, team owners and pit crews just as it is with any season. Among those new associations was rookie driver Jimmie Johnson and team owners Rick Hendrick and four-time NASCAR Winston Cup champion Jeff Gordon. When Johnson fired his engine for the first time during Speedweeks at Daytona in February of last year, there were no bands playing or fireworks exploding in the distance. Johnson was just another driver looking to make his mark on the ultra-competitive NASCAR Winston Cup circuit. Even though his blue and silver Chevrolet Monte Carlos carried the required rookie stripes on it's back bumper, the man behind the controls seemed anything but a competitor in his freshman season. It helped that he had Hendrick Motorsports equipment under him and Gordon, the winner of 61 Winston Cup races, offering support and advice.

Johnson showed he had enough talent to be considered for the ride. One could say Johnson came straight out of the desert to join the ranks of the NASCAR elite. From go-karts to off-road racing, he won six racing championships and three rookie of the year titles. Off-road racing deeply appealed to Johnson, but with Chevrolet's decision to cease funding for the series, he began to think of racing in other forms of motorsports. There was once a desire to drive Indy Cars, but stock cars had always been a favorite, even though it was prominent of the East coast and thousands of miles away.

He moved from his El Cajon, California home and headed east in hopes of starting the process of climbing up NASCAR's ladder. In 1998, he started three NASCAR Busch Series events and a year later, added two more to his schedule. In 2000, Johnson campaigned fulltime in the NASCAR Busch Series

Right: Jimmie Johnson's brown eyes peer intently through his racing helmet as he prepares to race at Lowe's Motor Speedway in May 2002. Johnson earned his third pole position of the year at the 600-mile Charlotte event.
Below: After just one season in Winston Cup racing, Johnson's silver-and-blue colors are well recognized around the circuit. Here he battles for position at Phoenix International Raceway in November.

in a bid for rookie honors. Even though he finished third in the rookie battle, he did finish 10th in the season-long point standings after starting 31 events. In 2001, Johnson scored his first win in a stock car in the inaugural Busch Series event at Chicagoland Speedway in Joliet, Illinois . Along with the win came four top-fives and nine top-10s and an eighth-place finish in the point standings. Hendrick and Gordon saw something in Johnson and offered him a contract as a NASCAR Winston Cup driver. The team owner and driver had so much confidence in him that they signed him before the start of the 2001 season and allowed him to fulfill his Busch Series commitment that year. The final piece of the puzzle was the hiring of Chad Knaus as the team's crew chief. Knaus had worked with Gordon as a crew member and showed he had the leadership skills to operate the race team in winning fashion. He and Johnson proved to be a strong and viable combination. In 2002, Johnson exceeded all expectations. He won three NASCAR Winston Cup events coming at Fontana, California and was twice a winner at Dover, Deleware. He logged four pole positions as well as six top-fives and 21 top-10s. Even though he fell short of Winston Cup Rookie of the Year honors to Ryan Newman, it was still a remarkable season.

Johnson was just as strong in 2003, winning races at Charlotte in May and New Hampshire in July and September, respectively. "We're building a team for the future," Johnson says. "The way this team has come together has gone past everyone's expectations. We just need to be polishing up our game and keep doing what we're doing and not put any extra pressures on ourselves. We've met all expectations at this point. Everything else is gravy. We want to gain experience so that we can be a championship threat in the years to come."

Top: Johnson celebrates his victory at Dover International Speedway in June 2002 with a smoky burnout in his Hendrick Motorsports Chevrolet. Left: Johnson's first career winner's trophy was earned at California Speedway in April.

Above: Shown here signing autographs for the fans at Indianapolis Motor Speedway in August 2002, Johnson quickly became a household name on the Winston Cup scene—and not simply for his matinee-idol good looks. Below: Johnson gets a hand from his Chad Knaus-led crew in pit row at Charlotte in May.

MATT KENSETH

17

Born:
March 10, 1972
Madison, Wisconsin

Height: 5-9

Weight: 152 lbs

Sponsor	DeWalt
Make	Ford
Crew Chief	Robbie Reiser
Owner	Jack Roush

Now that the 2003 NASCAR season is complete, Matt Kenseth, driver of the Roush Racing Ford, the Madison, Wisconsin native has a new title to add to his list of accomplishments. He is now a champion in NASCAR competition.

Kenseth gained the points lead in March of 2003 at Las Vegas after his win there and held it for the remainder of the 36-race season. Further, he did so with numbers so far ahead of the second-place finisher it would have taken having him sit out several races for anyone to have caught up.

Kenseth's driving career began when his father bought a racecar to drive and had his son maintain it with a few friends who helped on the crew. Once Matt reached his 16th birthday, the car was turned over to him. He progressed to the ARTGO Series and became its youngest winner (besting Winston Cup driver Mark Martin for that honor).

A large part of getting into the Winston Cup arena is getting noticed. Kenseth was hired by Jack Roush for the full 2000 Winston Cup season after five races with Roush in 1999. The young driver shocked the racing community by winning the Coca-Cola World 600 at Lowe's Motor Speedway in May that year. His 14th-place finish in the points standings was good enough to bring Kenseth the Rookie of the Year award in 2000.

After a winless 2001 campaign, Kenseth quickly asserted himself at the front of the pack in 2002. He claimed victory at Rockingham, North Carolina, in the second race of the season, captured another checkered flag at Texas Motor Speedway in April, and added a third trophy to the shelf with a win at Michigan in June.

NASCAR Winston Cup Career Statistics

Year	Races	Wins	Top 5s	Top 10s	Poles	Total Points	Final Standing	Winnings
1998	1	0	0	1	0	150	--	$42,340
1999	5	0	1	1	0	434	49th	$143,561
2000	34	1	4	11	0	3,711	14th	$2,408,138
2001	36	0	4	9	0	3,982	13th	$2,565,579
2002	36	5	11	19	1	4,432	8th	$3,888,850
2003	36	1	11	25	0	5,022	1st	$4,038,124
Totals	148	7	31	66	1	17,731		$13,086,592

Kenseth also scored victories at Richmond, Virginia in September and Phoenix, Arizona in November to become the winningest driver of the season.

"We've had a tremendous season in 2003," Kenseth says in his usual quiet tone. "It's been good but it's been a really long year."

"You have to be smart about winning a championship. You don't win them by making mistakes. We got here by doing things and having things work out for us. Some people say we've been lucky but I think you have to make your own luck. I've just told our guys on the crew to go out and do the very best we can. If we do that, the points will fall right into place."

Top: Matt Kenseth drove his DeWalt-sponsored Ford to a season-high five victories in 2002.

Left: Kenseth celebrates his first career NASCAR win in Charlotte's Victory Lane after the 600-mile event there in May 2000.

BOBBY LABONTE

18

Born:
May 8, 1964
Corpus Christi, Texas

Height: 5-9

Weight: 175 lbs

Sponsor	**Interstate Batteries**
Make	**Pontiac**
Crew Chief	**Michael McSwain**
Owner	**Joe Gibbs**

Quiet and determined, Bobby Labonte, driver of the Joe Gibbs Racing Chevrolets, is clearly on top of his game. His talent is coupled with that of crew chief Michael "Fatback" McSwaim and race cars that routinely go to the front. Consistent good finishes were enjoyed at the first of the 2003 season, but the pattern was not the same at the close of the season.

From all he has accomplished, one might reason that stock car racing is what Texas native Labonte is made of. Way back in 1984, a shy and rather young Bobby could be found over and underneath the Chevrolets that were being driven by older brother Terry. That year, the elder Labonte captured his first NASCAR Winston Cup championship. While Terry was accepting the trophy and all the checks, Bobby's mental wheels began turning toward putting his own racing career in motion.

Even before Terry's glory days with team owner Billy Hagan, Bobby followed in his brother's footsteps by fielding a quarter-midget racer at the mere age of five. Bobby continued to turn wrenches for Terry through

NASCAR Winston Cup Career Statistics

Year	Races	Wins	Top 5s	Top 10s	Poles	Total Points	Final Standing	Winnings
1991	2	0	0	0	0	110	--	$8,350
1993	30	0	0	6	1	3,221	19th	$395,660
1994	31	0	1	2	0	3,038	21st	$550,305
1995	31	3	7	14	2	3,718	10th	$1,413,682
1996	31	1	5	14	4	3,590	11th	$1,475,196
1997	32	1	9	18	3	4,101	7th	$2,217,999
1998	33	2	11	18	3	4,180	6th	$2,980,052
1999	34	5	23	26	5	5,061	2nd	$4,763,615
2000	34	4	19	24	2	5,130	1st	$7,361,386
2001	36	2	9	20	1	4,561	6th	$4,786,779
2002	36	1	5	7	0	3,810	16th	$3,851,770
2003	36	2	12	17	4	4,377	8th	$4,745,258
Totals	336	21	101	166	25	44,897		$34,550,052

Left: Bobby Labonte is at speed in his Joe Gibbs Racing Pontiac at Las Vegas in March 2002.

Right: Labonte enjoys a quiet moment while at Daytona in October 1998.

the 1986 season, but the following year he began his own Late Model Sportsman career, where he secured a track championship at Caraway Speedway with 12 victories and 7 pole positions in 23 races.

By 1990, Bobby Labonte's name was stenciled on the rooflines of the Busch Series Chevrolets he had sitting at his Trinity, North Carolina shop. He finished fourth in the season-long point standings that year, and came back in 1991 to win the NASCAR Busch Series championship. Obviously with that kind of success, there was no question Labonte was going to make a career of Winston Cup racing.

Early on, Bobby relied heavily on Terry for advice about which teams to sign with. There were times when Terry saved Bobby from

Above: Labonte enjoys a taste of victory at Pocono International Raceway in 1999. It was one of a career-high five wins that season. Below: The intensity can be seen in Labonte's eyes as he awaits the start of a race at Richmond in September 2000.

locking himself into teams that weren't championship caliber. By 1993, he found a home with Bill Davis Racing but lost Rookie of the Year honors to future Winston Cup champion Jeff Gordon. Having finished 19th and 21st in the point standings in his first two full seasons, Labonte was happy to take the ride with Joe Gibbs Racing when Dale Jarrett vacated the spot to join Robert Yates in 1995. Labonte won three races that season and set the stage for good things ahead. Since the beginning of Labonte's union with the former coach of the NFL Washington Redskins, record-breaking performances have been the standard for the team from Huntersville, North Carolina.

Labonte finished a strong second in the 1999 point standings and came back to win his own NASCAR Winston Cup championship in 2000. He collected 4 victories, including a win in the prestigious Brickyard 400, in his title year.

The 2003 season lacked consistency but Labonte is determined to get that back.

"We've had some great runs in 2003 and that's the ones I like to dwell on, not the ones we have fallen a bit short," Labonte says.

Right: Labonte proudly displays his Winston Cup championship trophy after clinching the title at Homestead, Florida, in November 2000. Below: Labonte's crew services the lime-green Pontiac at Talladega. Labonte is always a threat to win on the superspeedways.

TERRY LABONTE

5

Born:
November 16, 1956
Corpus Christi, Texas

Height: 5-10

Weight: 165 lbs

Sponsor	Kellogg's
Make	Chevrolet
Crew Chief	Jim Long
Owner	Rick Hendrick

On August 31, 2003, Terry Labonte, driver of the Hendrick Motorsports Chevrolet, enjoyed a long-awaited celebration in his favorite place—victory lane. It had been 156 races since Labonte could make that claim, but with only 33 laps remaining in the prestigious Southern 500, he took the lead and held it until he crossed under the checkered flag.

A two-time NASCAR Winston Cup champion, Labonte has performed on a variety of track configurations, but he would admit his career of late has been a roller-coaster ride. Still, after 23 years of highs and lows, the 45-year-old Texan still challenges the young guns in the drive for another championship.

Labonte's career began when team owner Billy Hagan picked him to drive his Winston Cup cars when Terry was only 22 years old and working as a crew member for Hagan. Labonte took over for Dick May in a race at Dover, Delaware, in September and brought Hagan's No. 92 Chevy home 10th. He also started five events in 1978, finishing in the top 10 three times, including a fourth place at Darlington Raceway in South Carolina, in his first career Winston Cup start. The Texas oilman had found his star. Although seat time was what Labonte needed most, sharing races with May allowed him to keep his rookie status for the following season.

Labonte and Hagan ditched the No. 92 for No. 44 at the start of the 1979 season, and solid, consistent finishes followed. Labonte made 31 starts that year and netted a 10th-place finish in the Winston Cup point standings. He fell just a few spots

NASCAR Winston Cup Career Statistics

Year	Races	Wins	Top 5s	Top 10s	Poles	Total Points	Final Standing	Winnings
1978	5	0	1	3	0	659	39th	$20,545
1979	31	0	2	13	0	3,615	10th	$130,057
1980	31	1	6	16	0	3,766	8th	$215,889
1981	31	0	8	17	2	4,052	4th	$334,987
1982	30	0	17	21	2	4,211	3rd	$363,970
1983	30	1	11	20	3	4,004	5th	$362,790
1984	30	2	17	24	2	4,508	1st	$713,010
1985	28	1	8	17	4	3,683	7th	$694,510
1986	29	1	5	10	1	3,473	12th	$522,235
1987	29	1	13	22	4	4,002	3rd	$825,369
1988	29	1	11	18	1	4,007	4th	$950,781
1989	29	2	9	11	0	3,564	10th	$704,806
1990	29	0	4	9	0	3,371	15th	$450,230
1991	29	0	1	7	1	3,024	18th	$348,898
1992	29	0	4	16	0	3,674	8th	$600,381
1993	30	0	0	10	0	3,280	18th	$531,717
1994	31	3	6	14	0	3,876	7th	$1,125,921
1995	31	3	14	17	1	4,146	6th	$1,558,659
1996	31	2	21	24	4	4,657	1st	$4,030,648
1997	32	1	8	20	0	4,177	6th	$2,270,144
1998	33	1	5	15	0	3,901	9th	$2,054,163
1999	34	1	1	7	0	3,580	12th	$2,475,365
2000	32	0	3	6	1	3,433	17th	$2,239,716
2001	36	0	1	3	0	3,280	23rd	$3,011,901
2002	36	0	1	4	0	3,417	24th	$3,143,990
2003	36	1	4	9	1	4,162	10th	$3,643,695
Totals	781	22	181	353	27	95,522		$33,324,377

During the 2001 Daytona 500, Terry Labonte found himself in a rather intense battle with teammate Jeff Gordon (No. 24) and Rusty Wallace (No. 2).

behind a young driver named Dale Earnhardt in the 1979 Rookie of the Year chase.

Labonte's love affair with Darlington continued at the 1980 Southern 500, where he collected his first Winston Cup victory—a win that still ranks among the biggest upsets in the race's history. Leaders David Pearson and Dale Earnhardt hit an oil slick in turn one, caused by Frank Warren's blown engine. Labonte trailed two seconds behind and won the race under caution.

The consistency continued, and in 1984 Labonte gave Hagan his only Winston Cup championship to date. From the outside, it looked as though relations between the champion driver and team owner were at an all-time high, but in the shadows, problems loomed. By 1987, Labonte moved over to Junior Johnson's organization, then one of the top teams on the tour. Limited success came with Johnson through 1989, as was the case with owner Richard Jackson in 1990. A surprise reunion with Hagan came in 1991, and the renewed partnership lasted through 1993. Following his 1984 title run, Labonte claimed only six victories over the next nine seasons, none of them with Jackson or Hagan.

Just as the critics turned up the assault, saying that Labonte was on the downhill slide—that glory had passed him by—an unexpected turn of events gave new life to his career. Ricky Rudd departed Hendrick Motorsports to start his own Winston Cup organization. Labonte's name surfaced as a possible replacement, and a strong finish at North Wilkesboro in late 1993 convinced team owner Rick Hendrick that Labonte was his man. The union with Hendrick has produced more victories for Labonte (eight) than with any other team owner, and led to a second Winston Cup title in 1996.

The pace slowed down after the second championship, with just one win per season from 1997 to 1999, and a winless 2000 and 2001. But Labonte continues on with Hendrick Motorsports, and the team feels confident in the potential for further success.

In March of 2002, Labonte reflects on another season ahead with Hendrick Motorsports.

By the spring of 2003, progress was beginning to surface. Good finishes were starting to find their way into the record books.

"We really started seeing a turnaround in our team about March of 2003 and it's gotten stronger from there," Labonte says. "Winning my second-career Southern 500 was just awesome. The night after the race, I couldn't sleep, so I went back in the livingroom to make sure the trophy was still there. It was a very special win for me.

"I think it's kind of neat, for me anyway, to have won my first race (at Darlington) and the last race there on Labor Day weekend. It's always been a pretty good place for me. Now that we've got another win, maybe more will come in the future."

Top: Labonte's Kellogg's-sponsored Chevy makes a scheduled pit stop at Texas Motor Speedway in April 2001. **Left:** Without the trademark mustache he sported for so many years, Labonte watches carefully as his crew prepares his car at Pocono in 1999. **Right:** According to Labonte, he couldn't have won at a better track than Texas, his home track, in March 1999.

STERLING MARLIN
40

Born:
June 30, 1957
Columbia, Tennessee

Height: 6-0

Weight: 180 lbs

Sponsor	**Coors Light**
Make	**Dodge**
Crew Chief	**Lee McCall**
Owner	**Chip Ganassi**

The sound of race engines roaring and welders crackling have filled Sterling Marlin's ears for as long as he can remember. Racing is a way of life for Sterling, just as it was for his dad, Clifton "Coo Coo" Marlin. Throughout Sterling's formative years, there was always a stock car of some type sitting in the shed out back. And after nearly three decades of racing in NASCAR, Marlin has never let fame and success taint his easygoing country personality.

At the age of 15, Marlin helped on his dad's pit crew during the summers, and occasionally the underage driver took the wheel of the transporter on the long trips from Columbia, Tennessee, to places like Michigan, Daytona, or Texas. When school was in session, Marlin worked on his dad's cars but stayed home to play football for his high school.

Marlin soon got the chance to fulfill his dream of driving stock cars. With help from his father's Winston Cup sponsor, H. B. Cunningham, the 16-year-old Marlin purchased a 1966 Chevelle to race at the Nashville Speedway. Soon after, in only his third start in a racecar, Marlin relieved his father in a Winston Cup event at Nashville on July 17, 1976. He finished eighth. A year later, he joined his father for his first superspeedway race, running an ARCA (American Race Car Association) car at Talladega.

NASCAR Winston Cup Career Statistics

Year	Races	Wins	Top 5s	Top 10s	Poles	Total Points	Final Standing	Winnings
1976	1	0	0	0	0	76	--	$565
1978	2	0	0	1	0	226	--	$10,170
1979	1	0	0	0	0	123	--	$505
1980	5	0	0	2	0	588	42nd	$29,810
1981	2	0	0	0	0	164	--	$1,955
1982	1	0	0	0	0	94	--	$4,015
1983	30	0	0	1	0	2,980	19th	$143,564
1984	14	0	0	2	0	1,207	37th	$54,355
1985	8	0	0	0	0	721	37th	$31,155
1986	10	0	2	4	0	989	36th	$113,070
1987	29	0	4	8	0	3,386	11th	$306,412
1988	29	0	6	13	0	3,621	10th	$521,464
1989	29	0	4	13	0	3,422	12th	$473,267
1990	29	0	5	10	0	3,387	14th	$369,167
1991	29	0	7	16	2	3,839	7th	$633,690
1992	29	0	6	13	5	3,603	10th	$649,048
1993	30	0	1	8	0	3,355	15th	$628,835
1994	31	1	5	11	1	3,443	14th	$1,127,683
1995	31	3	9	22	1	4,361	3rd	$2,253,502
1996	31	2	5	10	0	3,682	8th	$1,588,425
1997	32	0	2	6	0	2,954	25th	$1,301,370
1998	32	0	0	6	0	3,530	13th	$1,350,161
1999	34	0	2	5	1	3,397	16th	$1,797,416
2000	34	0	1	7	0	3,363	19th	$1,992,301
2001	36	2	12	20	1	4,741	3rd	$4,517,634
2002	29	2	8	14	2	3,703	18th	$3,711,150
2003	36	0	0	11	0	3,745	18th	$3,960,809
Totals	604	10	79	203	13	68,700		$27,571,498

Sterling Marlin's silver Dodge often ran near the front of the pack during 2002, until an injury sidelined him for the last seven races of the season. Here he is shown at Darlington Raceway in March.

Marlin continued on the short tracks and won three consecutive track championships at the Nashville Speedway in 1980, 1981, and 1982. He campaigned the full Winston Cup schedule in 1983 and went on to win Rookie of the Year honors driving for Roger Hamby.

Marlin struggled with various team owners until 1986, when he joined Billy Hagan for four full seasons. Two more seasons with Junior Johnson and one with Stavola Brothers Racing set the stage for his greatest successes, with Morgan-McClure Racing and later with Chip Ganassi.

After nearly 300 starts and nine second-place finishes, Marlin earned his first Winston Cup victory at the 1994 Daytona 500. He defended his Daytona 500 crown the following year, making him only the third driver in history to claim back-to-back Daytona 500 triumphs. Four more victories followed with McClure in 1995 and 1996: two at Talladega, one at Darlington, and a July win at Daytona.

After four winless seasons, Marlin rebounded with new team owner Ganassi in 2001, capturing two checkered flags and the third-place spot in the final points standings. The 2002 campaign started off well, with Marlin taking, and holding, the top spot in the point standings for 25 events on the schedule. He solidified his lead with victories at Las Vegas and Darlington in March, and by finishing in the top 10 in 8 of the first 10 races. A potentially serious neck injury sidelined him for the final seven events. Still, he remained optimistic.

He returned in 2003 but went winless through the first 30 events.

"All the guys on our crew do such a good job with the race cars and Ernie Elliott with the motors," Marlin says. "You hated for all of them when things go wrong on Sunday. But we're just going to keep digging and put together some good finishes and hopefully a win or two."

Marlin is all smiles as he strolls down pit road at Martinsville in October 2001.

Above: At Atlanta Motor Speedway in March 2001, Marlin does battle with teammate Casey Atwood. Below: Marlin's victory at Michigan in August 2001 was the first for Dodge in NASCAR Winston Cup competition since 1977. Right: Though he is often quiet when he's outside of his racecar, Marlin makes a lot of noise on the racetracks of Winston Cup.

MARK MARTIN

6

Born:
January 9, 1959
Batesville, Arkansas

Height: 5-6

Weight: 135 lbs

Sponsor	**Pfizer/Viagra**
Make	**Ford**
Crew Chief	**Ben Leslie**
Owner	**Jack Roush**

Mark Martin's game plan is usually pretty simple: If the win doesn't come, a strong finish in the top five will have to do. But Martin is also a realist and realizes just how hard winning NASCAR Winston Cup events can be. The competition gets tougher with each passing season.

Still, Martin finds a way to meet that challenge, as he has finished in the top-five point standings on 10 occasions and the top-10 in points 13 times.

Even when he was racing as a teenager back in the early 1970s, Martin was no different. He battled veteran drivers such as Bobby Allison, Dick Trickle, and Jim Sauter for American Speed Association (ASA) victories. Long before he was of legal age, Martin mastered the tracks of the Midwest better than some with twice the experience. He racked up hundreds of wins in addition to four ASA championships.

Martin took his winning ways to the Winston Cup arena in 1981, using a couple of his own Buick Regals. He scored two pole positions that year, one top 5, and one top 10. The strong start grabbed the attention of more than one team owner, but Martin again fielded his own team for the full schedule in 1982. He came up short to Geoff Bodine in the Rookie of the Year race, and fell short to the bank for the many dollars spent. His only chance to survive was as a hired gun for an owner hoping to make it big.

What followed was bittersweet. Team owner J. D. Stacy hired Martin in 1983 for what was to be a full schedule of racing. However, after only seven races, including a third-place finish at Darlington, Stacy fired Martin, a move that remains a mystery to some.

NASCAR Winston Cup Career Statistics

Year	Races	Wins	Top 5s	Top 10s	Poles	Total Points	Final Standing	Winnings
1981	5	0	1	2	2	615	42nd	$13,950
1982	30	0	2	8	0	3,181	14th	$126,655
1983	16	0	1	3	0	1,621	30th	$99,655
1986	5	0	0	0	0	488	48th	$20,515
1987	1	0	0	0	0	46	--	$3,550
1988	29	0	3	10	1	3,142	15th	$223,630
1989	29	1	14	18	6	4,053	3rd	$1,019,250
1990	29	3	16	23	3	4,404	2nd	$1,302,958
1991	29	1	14	17	5	3,914	6th	$1,039,991
1992	29	2	10	17	1	3,887	6th	$1,000,571
1993	30	5	12	19	5	4,150	3rd	$1,657,662
1994	31	2	15	20	1	4,250	2nd	$1,628,906
1995	31	4	13	22	4	4,320	4th	$1,893,519
1996	31	0	14	23	4	4,278	5th	$1,887,396
1997	32	4	16	24	3	4,681	3rd	$2,532,484
1998	33	7	22	26	3	4,964	2nd	$4,309,006
1999	34	2	19	26	1	4,943	3rd	$3,509,744
2000	34	1	13	20	0	4,410	8th	$3,098,874
2001	36	0	3	15	2	4,095	12th	$3,797,006
2002	36	1	12	22	0	4,762	2nd	$5,279,400
2003	36	0	5	10	0	3,769	17th	$4,048,847
Totals	566	33	205	325	41	73,973		$38,493,569

Mark Martin hits the concrete at Las Vegas Motor Speedway in March 2002. A third-place finish there helped Martin to a second-place finish in the season-long point standings.

For the remainder of the 1983 season and over the next few years, Martin picked up rides wherever he could, first with D. K. Ulrich, then in five events with J. Gunderman in 1986, and one event for Roger Hamby in 1987. It was a tough existence. Then came the break of a lifetime.

Automotive engineer Jack Roush was forming a Winston Cup team and needed an experienced driver. Martin got word that a search was on, and he convinced Roush to hire him. Money was never a consideration. His only desire was to be back with an established team in Winston Cup competition.

At the start of the 1988 season, Roush recognized Martin's burning desire to win and hired him over a long list of applicants. The first victory came on October 22, 1989, at North Carolina Motor Speedway in Rockingham. Since then, Martin and Roush have scored 17 more victories and 29 pole positions, and established themselves as winners in the NASCAR Busch Series.

Above: Martin is helmeted and ready to do battle before the start of an event at North Carolina Speedway in Rockingham. Right: Martin is in deep discussion with team owner Jack Roush prior to the start of the 500-mile event at Talladega Superspeedway in October 2001.

Top Left: Martin proved in October 1998 that he could still get the job done. Here he stands as the winner of the 500-mile event at Charlotte. Top Right: Martin has driven the No. 6 Ford for most of his Winston Cup career, and the pit crew has been crucial to the team's success. Bottom Left: Martin addresses fans and the media prior to the start of the Daytona 500 in February 1998. Bottom Right: Martin sits idle in the garage area at Las Vegas in 1998, reflecting on what he has to do to get a win there. A day later, he enjoyed the spoils of victory.

Although the wins have dwindled in recent years, the 33 career victories Martin has collected rank him 17th on the all-time win list.

"We've had some pretty fast cars despite the fact we've had some tough breaks," Martin says. "We have a team that is dedicated to getting this thing back on track and a group of guys who are the best and won't rest until the job is done. Everyone on this team is giving 100 percent."

JEREMY MAYFIELD

19

Born:
May 27, 1969
Owensboro, Kentucky

Height: 6-0

Weight: 190 lbs

Sponsor	**Dodge Dealers**
Make	**Dodge**
Crew Chief	**Sammy Johns**
Owner	**Ray Evernham**

There must be something in the water around Owensboro, Kentucky. Jeremy Mayfield, driver of the Evernham Motorsports Dodge, joins a long list of drivers who hail from that Southern town, including the three Green brothers (David, Mark, and Jeff) and the Waltrips (Michael and three-time champ Darrell). Whatever the reason, Mayfield certainly has the talent to make big things happen racing against his fellow Owensboro natives.

Like so many southern stock car drivers, Mayfield began his career as a go-kart racer and eventually moved through the ranks of Street Stocks, Sportsman, and Late Models. Winning the 1987 Rookie of the Year award at Kentucky Motor Speedway brought Mayfield one step closer to his dream of driving and winning at the NASCAR Winston

NASCAR Winston Cup Career Statistics

Year	Races	Wins	Top 5s	Top 10s	Poles	Total Points	Final Standing	Winnings
1993	1	0	0	0	0	76	--	$4,830
1994	20	0	0	0	0	1,673	37th	$226,265
1995	27	0	0	1	0	2,637	31st	$436,805
1996	30	0	2	2	1	2,721	26th	$592,853
1997	32	0	3	8	0	3,547	13th	$1,067,203
1998	33	1	12	16	1	4,157	7th	$2,332,034
1999	34	0	5	12	0	3,743	11th	$2,125,227
2000	32	2	6	12	4	3,307	24th	$2,169,251
2001	28	0	5	7	0	2,651	35th	$2,682,603
2002	36	0	2	4	0	3,309	26th	$2,494,580
2003	36	0	4	12	1	3,736	19th	$2,962,228
Totals	309	3	39	74	7	31,557		$17,093,879

Jeremy Mayfield at speed on the concrete racing surface at Dover, Delaware, in June 2002.

The Penske Racing team goes to work on Mayfield's Ford during a pit stop at Texas Motor Speedway in 2001. Mayfield drove for Penske before making the switch to Evernham's team.

Cup level. He became a regular on the ARCA circuit in 1993 and had finishes good enough to earn him his second rookie honor.

Mayfield finally made his Winston Cup debut at Charlotte in October 1993, driving for team owner Earl Sadler. Sadler had fielded cars for several notable up-and-coming drivers—including the late Davey Allison—so Mayfield appeared to be on the right path. He wheeled Sadler cars for four races in 1994, and T. W. Taylor also brought Mayfield on for four events that year. Then NASCAR legend Cale Yarborough called and asked for Mayfield's services. Many predicted it would be a prosperous marriage, but after 12 races in 1994 and a full season in 1995, the wins simply didn't come.

Late in the season in 1996, owners Yarborough and Michael Kranefuss swapped drivers. Mayfield went to work for Kranefuss while John Andretti went over to Yarborough's team. (Andretti won the 400-mile event at Daytona for Yarborough in 1997.)

After Kranefuss joined with racing legend Roger Penske, Mayfield had the best ride of his career. He scored wins at Pocono, Pennsylvania, in 1998 and 2000, as well as a win at California in 2000. In addition, there were pole positions at Darlington, Dover, Rockingham, Talladega, and Texas.

Despite the two wins, not all was well in 2000, as things slowly unraveled for the Penske-Mayfield partnership. When Mayfield's car was found to be too low after the California win, it seemed to mark the beginning of the end. Even though Mayfield had nothing to do with the height of the car, there was discord within the team. Finally, after additive was added to his gas tank by a crew member just before Mayfield's pole position run at Talladega, the end was all but written.

Apparently, both owner and driver wanted and needed a change after the tumultuous 2000 campaign. Mayfield finally got his wish the day after the inaugural event at Kansas Speedway in September

2001, when Penske Racing released Mayfield from his contract. From that day until the start of Speedweek 2002 that kicked off the new season, Mayfield sat on the sidelines waiting for a new ride. Finally, Evernham Motorsports came along, and a new relationship was formed.

He had not won a race with Evernham through the first 30 events of 2003 and received a great deal of criticism for not finding victory lane with such a stout organization. Mayfield, however, came very close with second-place finishes at Richmond, Virginia and Loudon, New Hampshire in the month of September. The late-season performances served as evidence things were finally coming together.

In post-race interviews at Richmond, Mayfield said, "This shows the potential (of the team) is there. These guys gave me what I needed and that's all I've ever asked for. We had a great run. It's pretty cool to know where we came from-both tonight and this season."

Above: Mayfield anticipates the start of the Winston Cup event at Las Vegas in March 2001. Left: Mayfield waves to the crowd during pre-race ceremonies prior to the start of the 600-mile event at Charlotte in May 2000.

JAMIE McMURRAY

42

Born:
June 3, 1976
Joplin, Missouri

Height: 5-6

Weight: 145 lbs

Sponsor	Havoline
Make	Dodge
Crew Chief	Donnie Wingo
Owner	Chip Ganassi and Felix Sabates

NASCAR Winston Cup Career Statistics

Year	Races	Wins	Top 5s	Top 10s	Poles	Total Points	Final Standing	Winnings
2003	36	0	5	13	1	3,965	13th	$2,699,969
Total	36	0	5	13	1	3,965		$2,699,969

When Jamie McMurray emerged onto the NASCAR Winston Cup circuit in late 2002, he proved that Cinderella finishes can unfold and dreams really do come true. Of the millions of fans and the close-knit NASCAR fraternity witnessing the conclusion of the 500-mile event at Lowe's Motor Speedway on October 13, McMurray was probably the most surprised of them all at the outcome.

To set the stage, veteran driver Sterling Marlin was injured in a crash at Kansas on September 29 and could not compete for the remainder of the season after leading the point standings for 25 consecutive weeks. Team owner Chip Ganassi had had his eye on McMurray as a possible third-team driver in 2003 but had not yet presented him a contract. McMurray started his tenure with the Mooresville, North Carolina based team at Talladega, Alabama, October 6 with a 26th-place finish. Most everyone thought this was going to be another story of a "NASCAR Busch Series gets a Winston Cup ride" only to need months to prove himself. Nothing could have been further from the truth.

McMurray thanked Ganassi for having confidence in him by rolling into victory lane after a long, hard fought battle with veteran Bobby Labonte in the 500-mile event at Charlotte. He became the fifth driver to win in just his second outing and the first in NASCAR's modern era (dating back to 1971).

What makes the story more incredible in the fact McMurray had gone winless in all other NASCAR divisions but waited to take his first triumph in the biggest stock car arena of them all.

"What has happened to me over the past year is really hard to describe,"

McMurray says. "Many great things have happened and the biggest thing would be the fact I was given the opportunity to drive these Chip Ganassi race cars. It's an awesome feeling, let me tell you.

McMurray's now has his name etched on the rooflines of his own black and silver No. 42 Dodges and looks to have a promising career in Winston Cup racing. "I can't thank (team owners) Chip Ganassi and Felix Sabates enough for taking a chance on me. It's been incredible with all that's happened."

Jamie McMurray, driver of the No. 42 Chip Ganassi Racing Dodge, turns in a near flawless lap during a qualifying at Martinsville (VA.) Speedway in April of 2003.

CASEY MEARS

41

Born:
March 12, 1978
Bakersfield, California

Height: 5-8

Weight: 158 lbs

Sponsor	Target
Make	Dodge
Crew Chief	Jimmy Elledge
Owner	Chip Ganassi

NASCAR Winston Cup Career Statistics

Year	Races	Wins	Top 5s	Top 10s	Poles	Total Points	Final Standing	Winnings
2003	36	0	0	0	0	2,638	35th	$2,639,178
Totals	36	0	0	0	0	2,638	35th	$2,639,178

Auto racing enthusiasts may notice that the name Casey Mears, driver of the Chip Ganassi Racing Dodge, seems familiar. He is the nephew of Rick Mears, a four-time winner of the Indianapolis 500. He is also the son of two-time Indianapolis 500 starter and off-road legend Roger Mears.

The younger Mears stuck with the family's tradition by winning his first feature event at Masa Marin in 1994 at the mere age of 16. From there, young Casey put together further impressive numbers.

By 2000, the speeds were getting quite a bit higher. He successfully completed his rookie test for the Indianapolis 500 in 2000. That same year, he finished third in the Indy Lights Series, scoring his first win at the Grand Prix of Houston.

No wins came to the young star in stock car racing but he did manage to gain quite a bit of experience racing against the likes of fellow teammates Jamie McMurray and

Sterling Marlin, as well as a virtual "Who's Who" of NASCAR stars.

"It hasn't gone the way we've wanted it to but its gotten better all the time," Mears says. "Anytime I've got a really good race car, something bad happens or if we have a decent car going for us, then I make a mistake or something. We just haven't put a good race together yet. Our OK races have been OK. We've haven't finished 15th, 16th, or 17th. We've had a lot of top-10s in our grasp. We just haven't finalized the deal. It's getting better as we go."

Opposite Page: Casey Mears, driver of the No. 41 Chip Ganassi Racing Dodge, contemplates the job at hand during a break from driving during his rookie season in 2003. Above: Mears rests his hands on his steering wheel as he awaits the command to fire his engine during one of 36 events he entered in 2003. Left: Mears leads teammate Sterling Marlin as they battle for track position in hopes of logging one of many impressive finishes.

JERRY NADEAU

36

Born:
September 9, 1970
Danbury, Connecticut

Height: 5-6

Weight: 150 lbs

Sponsor	U.S. Army
Make	Pontiac
Crew Chief	TBD
Owner	MB2 Motorsports

The gameplan of Jerry Nadeau, driver of the MB2 Motorsports Pontiac, was to get to know his new team and put together a string of race wins and pole positions. The MB2 Motorsports of Mooresville, North Carolina was excited to have a winning driver in their stable and optimism was high. What occurred instead was a serious accident at Richmond International Raceway on May 2, 2003 that placed him on the sidelines for the majority of the 36-race season. In the months that followed, Nadeau slowly recovered from head injuries that included lesions on the brain, a fractured shoulder as well as rib and lung injuries. Like taking small steps that lead to big ones, Nadeau had to learn how to walk and talk all over again.

In happier days, Nadeau got his start as a master of karting. He won 10 World Karting Association and International Karting Foundation championships between 1984 and 1990.

When Nadeau entered the world of NASCAR Winston Cup racing in 1997, he did so on a limited schedule with team owner Richard Jackson. In 1998, former champion Bill Elliott tapped Nadeau to wheel his cars. Although little success came from that venture, team owner Rick Hendrick saw Nadeau's raw talent. He moved to Hendrick's organization in 2000 and won the season-ending Winston Cup event at Atlanta Motor Speedway.

Nadeau was released from Hendrick Motorsports rather early into the 2002 season. After a stint with Petty Enterprises, he joined MB2 Motorsports for 2003. But Nadeau only completed 10 races before his serious accident at Richmond occurred.

On September 2, Nadeau returned to the Richmond area and visited with the doctors who worked to save his life.

NASCAR Winston Cup Career Statistics

Year	Races	Wins	Top 5s	Top 10s	Poles	Total Points	Final Standing	Winnings
1997	5	0	0	0	0	287	54th	$118,545
1998	30	0	0	0	0	2,121	36th	$804,867
1999	34	0	1	2	0	2,686	34th	$1,370,229
2000	34	1	3	5	0	3,273	20th	$2,164,778
2001	36	0	4	10	0	3,675	17th	$2,507,827
2002	28	0	0	1	0	2,250	37th	$1,801,760
2003	10	0	1	1	0	844	45th	$861,628
Totals	177	1	9	19	0	15,136		$9,629,634

"It was emotional," Nadeau said of his visit. Obviously you wanted to cry, but I was trying be macho about it and hold it in.

"I think it was more emotional for them. Half of the people I didn't even remember. I think it was more emotional for them considering they haven't seen me in three months and I was almost dead when they saw me. It was more inspirational just to go there and say hello to all the doctors that basically put me back together."

Opposite Page: Jerry Nadeau, driver of the MB2 Motorsports Pontiac, seems to be studying activity in the garage area during a break in the action. Above: Nadeau pushes the throttle of his MB2 Pontiac in one of only 10 starts with the team before an accident during qualifying at Richmond International Raceway in September of 2003 sidelined his career.

JOE NEMECHEK

25

Born:
September 26, 1963
Lakeland, Florida

Height: 5-9

Weight: 185 lbs

Sponsor	**UAW-Delphi**
Make	**Chevrolet**
Crew Chief	**Peter Sospenzo**
Owner	**Rick Hendrick**

For Joe Nemechek, the rule has always been that if it goes fast, it's ready to race. From the time Joe and his late brother John were old enough to reach the pedals on their bicycles, they dreamed of becoming stars in NASCAR. Sadly, at the age of 27, John Nemechek lost his life in an accident during a NASCAR Craftsman Truck Series event in March 1997.

From an early age, Joe Nemechek has had the word "champion" associated with his name. He began racing motocross at age 13, winning more than 300 trophies in six years, before entering the realm of short-track events in his native Florida in 1987.

Never one to do anything halfway, Nemechek won Rookie of the Year honors and championships in three straight years. He went on to take the NASCAR Busch Series championship in 1992 before officially joining the NASCAR Winston Cup ranks in 1993. To date, he is a two-time winner in Winston Cup and has collected nearly $10 million in earnings.

In 2002, Nemechek joined Hendrick Motorsports, replacing Jerry Nadeau. The result late in the season showed promising results with crew chief Peter Sospenzo.

In 2003, Nemechek and Sospenzo pulled off a strong victory at Richmond, Virginia on May 3. Even so, the 10-year veteran lost his ride with Hendrick to make way for the younger NASCAR Busch Series standout Brian Vickers.

"Rick (Hendrick) is doing everything he can to help me land a good, quality ride for next year," Nemechek says. "Rick had to start pulling all the resources he could and GMAC (Vickers NASCAR Busch Series sponsor) said they'd step up. It's a great opportunity for Brian Vickers."

NASCAR Winston Cup Career Statistics

Year	Races	Wins	Top 5s	Top 10s	Poles	Total Points	Final Standing	Winnings
1993	5	0	0	0	0	389	44th	$56,580
1994	29	0	1	3	0	2,673	27th	$389,565
1995	29	0	1	4	0	2,742	28th	$428,925
1996	29	0	0	2	0	2,391	34th	$666,247
1997	30	0	0	3	2	2,754	28th	$732,194
1998	32	0	1	4	0	2,897	26th	$1,343,991
1999	34	1	1	3	3	2,956	30th	$1,634,946
2000	34	0	3	9	1	3,534	15th	$2,105,042
2001	31	1	1	4	0	2,994	28th	$2,510,723
2002	33	0	3	3	0	2,682	34th	$2,453,020
2003	36	1	2	6	0	3,426	25th	$2,560,484
Totals	322	3	13	41	6	29,438		$14,881,717

Above: Joe Nemechek took over the UAW-Delphi Chevrolet for Hendrick Motorsports in 2002.

Left: Nemechek celebrates a surprise win at New Hampshire Speedway in September 1999.

RYAN NEWMAN

12

Born:
December 8, 1977
South Bend, Indiana

Height: 5-11

Weight: 207 lbs

Sponsor
Alltel
Make
Ford
Crew Chief

Ever If Ryan Newman, driver of the Penske Racing Dodge proved anything in 2003 it was that engineers can win stock car races. The Purdue University graduate by far sealed the win category with eight wins through the Oct. 5 event at Kansas Speedway and threatened to win a few more before the season was complete.

Newman also had another impressive notation in his resume; he was also successful in the lighter, lightning fast open wheel machines.

Ever since Rick Hendrick discovered Jeff Gordon within the open-wheel Sprint Car ranks, other team owners have scoured the Sprint grids for potential future champions. When team owners Roger Penske, Don Miller, and Rusty Wallace went out looking for new talent, they discovered Ryan Newman, a 24-year-old open-wheel star who is already in the Quarter Midget Hall of Fame.

Having been named to Penske's organization carried a huge amount of clout, as Penske is known in several forms of auto racing around the world for have the best equipment, and talent, money can buy. Having the endorsement of Wallace, the 1989 NASCAR Winston Cup champion, made acceptance in the garage area a bit easier. From there, Newman would slowly gain their respect on and off the race track.

Newman graduated from Purdue University with a degree in Vehicular Structural Engineering, something that might come in handy when setting up some of the Winston Cup machines. He pulled off wins in ARCA (Automobile Racing Club of America) competition at Pocono, Kentucky Speedway, and Charlotte. He was also victorious in all three USAC divisions: midgets, sprint cars, and the Silver Bullet Series.

Newman competed in both the Winston Cup and Busch Series in 2001, and his

NASCAR Winston Cup Career Statistics

Year	Races	Wins	Top 5s	Top 10s	Poles	Total Points	Final Standing	Winnings
2000	1	0	0	0	0	40	--	$37,825
2001	7	0	2	2	1	652	49th	$465,276
2002	36	1	14	22	6	4,593	6th	$4,373,830
2003	36	8	17	22	11	4,711	6th	$4,827,377
Totals	80	9	33	46	18	9,996		$9,704,308

Right: Focus and determination put Ryan Newman alongside savvy veterans during his Rookie of the Year campaign in 2002. Below: The young Newman has quickly made a name for himself in his Penske Racing Ford. At Darlington in March 2002 he earned a fifth-place finish, one of 14 top fives on the year.

impact on the scene was almost immediate. In only his third career Winston Cup start, he scored a pole position in the 600-mile event at Charlotte. In seven starts that season, Newman kept his Penske Racing Ford up front on several occasions. He grabbed a fifth-place finish at Michigan in June, and topped that with a second-place running, behind Jeff Gordon, at Kansas Speedway's inaugural race in September.

In 2002, Newman won at Loudon, New Hampshire and collected that elusive first NASCAR Winston Cup victory. Even though weather dictated NASCAR's decision to red-flag the event in its late stages, the win was still his. So many within the sport had predicted, without a doubt, he would win Winston Cup events. Even more insiders predicted he will continue to score victories each season and establish himself as a rising superstar. All one has to do is look at his 2002 statistics of 14 top-fives and 22 top-10s to see his rise to the top is quickly developing.

Those numbers also proved to be the foundation for winning 2002 Rookie of the Year honors. After a hard-fought battle with Jimmie Johnson, driver of the Hendrick Motorsports Chevrolet, Newman's smoothness behind the wheel of his race cars and behind the microphone during interviews proved he had the charisma to represent NASCAR well.

In 2003, Newman certainly showed the veteran drivers how to get the job done.

"This is absolutely race team and I wouldn't have the wins I have without them. Matt Borland (crew chief) and the entire team worked hard to keep us out front and winning races."

"Our team is no different than anybody else. We've got a great bunch of guys. That to me is the difference as far as their character. Things happen to everybody. It's who can fight through it the best, and they've done a great job of doing that."

Top Left: The concentration shown on Newman's face helps explain his success on the track, where focus is essential. Above Right: Although he finished sixth in the overall standings, Newman claimed just one winner's trophy during the 2002 season. It came at New Hampshire International Speedway in September, and was the first of his young career. Below Left: Newman's rapid rise to the top made him the target of many interviewers during his stellar rookie campaign. Below Right: Newman gets service from his crew during the NAPA Auto Parts 500 at California Speedway in April 2002.

STEVE PARK

30

Born:
August 23, 1967
East Northport, New York

Height: 6-2

Weight: 190 lbs

Sponsor
AOL
Make
Chevrolet
Crew Chief

When Dale Earnhardt was looking for a driver to wheel his Chevrolets in the Busch Series for the team he was developing, Dale Earnhardt Inc., he needed a hot shoe who was young and hungry to win. He placed his confidence in Steve Park, a driver who went on to show his famous employer that he could win in Winston Cup competition as well. Park began racing in the northeastern United States, following in the footsteps of his father, Bob Park, a winning modified driver in the region for many years. Now Bob Park drives modifieds in the New York area in cars owned by his famous son, Steve.

From the ARCA division to the NASCAR Featherlite Modified Series in 1995, Steve Park put together a program good enough to finish second in the season-long points battle. When he won three times and took Rookie of the Year honors in Earnhardt's car in 1997, he was already being talked about as a promising Winston Cup star.

Since entering the Winston Cup arena in 1998, Park's career has been one of feast or famine. Before he could even get his career going, he crashed during a practice session at Atlanta Motor Speedway and suffered a severely broken leg that caused him to miss 15 of the scheduled 34 events. He came back to finish 11th at Michigan Speedway in August of that year, and again at Dover Downs a month later.

In 2000, Park broke into Victory Lane by winning at Watkins Glen, the track he considers his home track. One of Park's most special moments was having Earnhardt greet him in Victory Lane after he stood on top of his yellow and black Chevrolet.

A year later, Park seemed to be on the fast track to success. Just one week after

NASCAR Winston Cup Career Statistics

Year	Races	Wins	Top 5s	Top 10s	Poles	Owner Total Points	Final Standing	Winnings
1997	5	0	0	0	0	326	51st	$74,480
1998	17	0	0	0	0	1,322	42nd	$487,265
1999	34	0	0	5	0	3,481	14th	$1,767,690
2000	34	1	6	13	2	3,934	11th	$2,283,629
2001	24	1	5	12	0	2,859	32nd	$2,385,971
2002	32	0	0	2	0	2,694	33rd	$2,681,590
2003	35	0	1	3	2	2,923	32nd	$2,686,915
Totals	146	2	11	32	2	14,616		$9,680,625

Steve Park's yellow-and-black No. 1 machine is familiar to NASCAR fans. Here he passes the grandstands at Martinsville Speedway in April 2002.

Earnhardt lost his life on the final lap of the Daytona 500, Park scored a photo-finish victory over Bobby Labonte at Rockingham. He followed that up with 11 more top-10 finishes, including second places at Darlington, Texas, and Dover Downs.

Twenty-four races into the season, Park was sitting in 10th place in the Winston Cup point standings when he was involved in a freak accident during a Busch Series event. Crew members within the sport speculate that the steering wheel on Park's Chevrolet was not properly attached by the standard pin that secured it to the steering column. The wheel came off in his hands and with-

out control of the car, he was T-boned in the driver's side by Larry Foyt, who was moving up to his proper starting position on the inside line as a lapped car.

Park suffered head injuries in the crash, requiring many months of slow recovery. The results after the crash were not as good and he or his team had expected. Both team and driver continued to hope for future success.

Finally, by the time the circuit reached the 600-mile event at Charlotte, North Carolina in May of 2003, Park was offered a ride with powerhouse team owner Richard Childress. The union produced pole posi-

Park ponders the race ahead at Dover Downs in June 2000.

tions at Fontana, California in April and Daytona Beach in July and scored one top-five and three top-10s through Kansas. Still, the driver and team owner elected to part ways at season's end.

"I've had a great experience with RCR and Richard has been very supportive throughout our relationship," Park says. "I greatly appreciate him giving me the opportunity to drive for his organization this season," stated Park. "I feel that I am in the best physical shape I have ever been and I know that I still have a lot to look forward to as a winning driver."

Above: Suited up and ready for action, Park is focused behind the wheel of his DEI Chevrolet Monte Carlo at Darlington in September 2000. Below Left: The DEI crew works fast to keep Park's ride running smoothly. Below Right: Park studies the winding road course at Watkins Glen. In August 2000, he scored his first career Winston Cup victory there.

KYLE PETTY

Born:
June 2, 1960
Trinity, North Carolina

Height: 6-2

Weight: 195 lbs

Sponsor
Georgia-Pacific
Make
Dodge
Crew Chief

When your last name is Petty and your father is known as "The King" of stock car racing, your career is pretty much pre-ordained. Even before he ever drove a racecar, Kyle Petty was being touted as a star of the future. He was the talk of racing circles at home and abroad. Surely he would be a chip off the old block, they said.

As a child, Kyle saw stock car racing as nothing more than his father's profession. The cars in the nearby shop were shiny blue with painted numbers on their doors, set up to be turned left around short tracks and superspeedways. He was surrounded by the sounds of air grinders hitting metal and engines screaming on the dynamometer.

Kyle at first resisted the seemingly pre-determined path to the oval track during his adventurous and trouble-filled teenage years, but he eventually turned his energies toward his destiny. To become a Winston Cup racer was a tough but reasonable goal for any young driver. To meet the high expectations that come with bearing the Petty name, under the intense scrutiny of the press and public, was a much different story.

At the start of Speedweek in 1979, Petty came to Daytona International Speedway with a Dodge Magnum, a discarded Winston Cup machine his father had used with no success the year before. Although it had a heavy box-like design, the car was perfect for the younger Petty, who entered it in ARCA competition.

Miraculously, Kyle met the media expectations right off the bat. He won the ARCA 200 in his first outing on a closed course. For a brief time, he was the only undefeated stock car driver in America.

His career launched, a total of 169 races passed before Petty found Victory Lane in Winston Cup competition. It came

NASCAR Winston Cup Career Statistics

Year	Races	Wins	Top 5s	Top 10s	Poles	Total Points	Final Standing	Winnings
1979	5	0	0	1	0	559	37th	$10,810
1980	15	0	0	6	0	1,690	28th	$36,350
1981	31	0	1	10	0	3,335	12th	$112,289
1982	29	0	2	4	0	3,024	15th	$120,730
1983	30	0	0	2	0	3,261	13th	$157,820
1984	30	0	1	6	0	3,159	16th	$324,555
1985	28	0	7	12	0	3,523	9th	$296,367
1986	29	1	4	14	0	3,537	10th	$403,242
1987	29	1	6	14	0	3,732	7th	$544,437
1988	29	0	2	8	0	3,296	13th	$377,092
1989	19	0	1	5	0	2,099	30th	$117,022
1990	29	1	2	14	2	3,501	11th	$746,326
1991	18	1	2	4	2	2,078	31st	$413,727
1992	29	2	9	17	3	3,945	5th	$1,107,063
1993	30	1	9	15	1	3,860	5th	$914,662
1994	31	0	2	7	0	3,339	15th	$806,332
1995	30	1	1	5	0	2,638	30th	$698,875
1996	28	0	0	2	0	2,696	27th	$689,041
1997	32	0	2	9	0	3,455	15th	$984,314
1998	33	0	0	2	0	2,675	30th	$1,287,731
1999	32	0	0	9	0	3,103	26th	$1,278,953
2000	19	0	0	1	0	1,441	41st	$894,911
2001	24	0	0	0	0	1,673	43rd	$1,008,919
2002	36	0	0	1	0	3,501	22nd	$1,995,820
2003	33	0	0	0	0	2,414	37th	$2,293,222
Totals	645	8	51	168	8	69,120		$15,327,388

Kyle Petty at speed at Darlington in September 2001. The one-groove racetrack isn't one of Petty's favorites. He once jokingly suggested it be filled with water and minnows for fishing.

Kyle Petty, driver of the No.45 Petty Enterprises

Dodge, is widely known for his easy, trademark smile.

in 1986, at the short track in Richmond, Virginia, with the Wood Brothers team. The win established him as the first third-generation driver to win a Winston Cup race. His grandfather, Lee, won his first race in 1949, and his father, Richard, first stood on the top spot in 1960. Kyle notched another win in 1987 at the Coca-Cola 600, his first superspeedway triumph.

Six more wins followed with team owner Felix Sabates, but the Cuban transplant and the North Carolina country boy parted ways in 1996 after eight seasons together. They had become as close as father and son, but the results on the track didn't warrant another year together.

Petty elected to field his own cars in 1997 and 1998, meeting only limited success. In 1999, he reopened Petty Enterprises, partly to field cars for his son Adam in the Busch Series and, eventually, Winston Cup. That dream came to a tragic end when young Adam was killed in a single-car accident during a practice session at New Hampshire International Raceway on

May 12, 2000. Since his son's death, Petty has campaigned the colors, sponsors, and number Adam used in Busch Series competition and his lone Winston Cup start at Texas Motor Speedway two weeks before his death. It is in memory of his son that Kyle hopes to bring Petty Enterprises back to winning form.

"The most frustrating part of it for me is that we haven't moved forward on the race track," Petty said in NASCAR Illustrated. "I'm not going to say that about things off the race track. Off the race track, our aero (aerodynamics) program has moved forward, our engineering has moved forward, and the structure we have at Petty Enterprises has moved forward by leaps and bounds."

"On the race track, we have lacked the performance we need. That's been the frustrating part because last year, we moved forward a little bit. We didn't make huge strides, but we moved forward substantially from where we were. We just haven't been able to maintain that momentum."

Above: In the garage area at Daytona in 1998, Petty stands in front of one of the Petty Enterprises toolboxes that carries the familiar Petty decals. Below: Just four months after his son, Adam, lost his life in a crash during a Busch Series practice session, Petty began driving his son's racecar in Adam's sponsors' colors. Here, Petty gets ready for an event at Darlington in September 2000.

RICKY RUDD

Born:
September 12, 1956
Chesapeake, Virginia

Height: 5-8

Weight: 160 lbs

21

Sponsor	
Motorcraft	
Make	
Ford	
Crew Chief	

icky Rudd's youthful face has been seen in Victory Lane at least once every season for 17 years, making him one of the most consistent drivers on the Winston Cup circuit. Along with his wins have come many pole positions and more than $24 million in career earnings.

Rudd began racing motocross and go-karts at a very early age but didn't drive a stock car until he first sat down in a Winston Cup ride in 1975 at age 18. He took four starts that year with Bill Champion, and one top-10 finish foretold Rudd's potential. In 1976, he started four more events, this time in cars fielded by his father, Al Rudd Sr., and reeled off another top-10 finish—a hint of the consistency that would mark his lengthy career. With his family-owned team, Rudd tackled the majority of the schedule in 1977, competing in 25 events, and earned Rookie of the Year honors after finishing 17th in the point standings that season.

Rudd came back to start in 13 races in 1978, garnering results sufficient to land a ride with longtime team owner Junie Donlavey for the full schedule in 1979. He scored two third-place finishes and two fifths in 1979, earning him nearly $150,000. Overall, it was a good learning season for Rudd.

In 1980, back with the Rudd family operation for 13 events, Ricky found himself in a make-or-break situation. Money was running out fast, but one good race could get him noticed by the better-financed teams on the circuit, providing perhaps his only chance to remain an active driver. That October, Rudd entered the National 500 at Charlotte Motor Speedway in a year-old car and qualified on the outside front row. By race's end, Rudd was fourth, finishing behind legends Dale Earnhardt, Cale Yarborough, and Buddy Baker. As hoped, the

NASCAR Winston Cup Career Statistics

Year	Races	Wins	Top 5s	Top 10s	Poles	Total Points	Final Standing	Winnings
1975	4	0	0	1	0	431	53rd	$4,345
1976	4	0	0	1	0	407	56th	$7,525
1977	25	0	1	10	0	2,810	17th	$68,448
1978	13	0	0	4	0	1,264	32nd	$49,610
1979	28	0	4	17	0	3,642	9th	$146,302
1980	13	0	1	3	0	1,319	32nd	$50,500
1981	31	0	14	17	3	3,991	6th	$381,968
1982	30	0	6	13	2	3,542	9th	$201,130
1983	30	2	7	14	4	3,693	9th	$257,585
1984	30	1	7	16	4	3,918	7th	$476,602
1985	28	1	13	19	0	3,857	6th	$512,441
1986	29	2	11	17	1	3,823	5th	$671,548
1987	29	2	10	13	0	3,742	6th	$653,508
1988	29	1	6	11	2	3,547	11th	$410,954
1989	29	1	7	15	0	3,608	8th	$534,824
1990	29	1	8	15	2	3,601	7th	$573,650
1991	29	1	9	17	1	4,092	2nd	$1,093,765
1992	29	1	9	18	1	3,735	7th	$793,903
1993	30	1	9	14	0	3,644	10th	$752,562
1994	31	1	6	15	1	4,050	5th	$1,044,441
1995	31	1	10	16	2	3,734	9th	$1,337,703
1996	31	1	5	16	0	3,845	6th	$1,503,025
1997	32	2	6	11	0	3,330	17th	$1,975,981
1998	33	1	1	5	0	3,131	22nd	$1,602,895
1999	34	0	3	5	1	2,922	31st	$1,632,011
2000	34	0	12	19	2	4,575	5th	$2,974,970
2001	36	2	14	22	1	4,706	4th	$4,878,027
2002	36	1	8	12	1	4,323	10th	$4,009,380
2003	36	0	4	5	0	3,521	23rd	$3,106,614
Totals	767	23	187	356	28	93,282		$28,599,603

Budweiser 400 in Riverside, California. Over the next few years, Rudd won six races driving for Bud Moore, two more with Kenny Bernstein, and captured four wins and a second-place finish in the 1991 Winston Cup point championship with Rick Hendrick. Since then, he has scored more victories with his own team and with Robert Yates, a longtime friend he joined at the start of the 2000 season.

Since entering the Winston Cup circuit, Rudd's name has surfaced each season as a driver who is a constant threat for victory. With the Yates organization, Rudd had longtime members of the press believing that he would return to championship status. That may come this season with Rudd's new operation, a team that's been around for over 50 years.

"I guess I would have to divide it up in segments. If I look at the first half of the season on a scale of one to 10, I'd have to put us down about a three or a four, meaning, not real pleased," Rudd says. "If I rate our performance in recent weeks, I would put it up around an eight with a second and a third and an 11th at Dover. There's a big difference in the first part of the season and this last of the season stretch we're in right now.

impressive run caught the notice of several veteran team owners.

Rudd signed with Digard Racing for the 1981 season, replacing Darrell Waltrip. Even though the results from the Digard-Rudd union weren't overly impressive, there were definite signs of promise.

Rudd switched to the Richard Childress team in 1982, and his first Winston Cup victory came the following year at the

Above: Rudd campaigned several paint schemes during the 2003 season. Here he is shown in a Ford supported by the United States Air Force. Right: Rudd makes a pit stop while using a car that a featured a paint scheme designed by his 10-year old son, Landon.

Above: Ricky Rudd, driver of the Wood Brothers Racing Ford, moves through one of the slightly banked turns at the famed half-mile Martinsville (VA.) Speedway. Left: Rudd is focused behind the wheel of his Robert Yates Racing Ford at Rockingham in February 2002.

ELLIOTT SADLER

38

Born:
April 30, 1975
Emporia, Virginia

Height: 6-2

Weight: 195 lbs

Sponsor
M&M/Mars
Make
Ford
Crew Chief

Elliott Sadler has enjoyed going fast since a young age. He began racing go-karts at age seven. By the time he turned to stock cars at the age of 18, he had compiled the same winning record as Richard Petty.

Before long, the urge to take his racing to a higher level brought Sadler to NASCAR's Busch Series. In 76 starts in the series, Sadler logged five victories and 12 top fives. His standout abilities caught the attention of brothers Len and Eddie Wood in 1999.

Wood Brothers Racing and the number they campaign are storied legends in NASCAR.

Sadler showed early in his Winston Cup career that he has the talent to follow in the footsteps of the great drivers of the past such as Marvin Panch, Chris Turner and David Pearson. He quickly repaid the Wood brothers' confidence in him with a win at Bristol Motor Speedway in April 2001.

In 2003, Sadler joined Robert Yates Racing and enjoyed some promising finishes. Victory lane, however, had eluded him through the first 30 events last season. The Virginia native also endured his share of scary crashes, one of which featured him flipping end over end at Talladega Superspeedway at the end of October.

"We've had our ups and downs and I wouldn't call it a real successful season, but we have had a lot of changes within the team with a couple of different crew chiefs and car chiefs and things like that," Sadler says. "There were changes that we didn't expect to have happen. Things that we think will help the whole Robert Yates organization in the near future and years to come. If there are any bad luck situations, we definitely get caught on the raw end of the deal. We're making the most of it. We just need to work on it and build on it and hopefully be a little better next year."

NASCAR Winston Cup Career Statistics

Year	Races	Wins	Top 5s	Top 10s	Poles	Total Points	Final Standing	Winnings
1998	2	0	0	0	0	128	--	$45,325
1999	34	0	0	1	0	3,191	24th	$1,589,221
2000	33	0	0	1	0	2,762	29th	$1,578,356
2001	36	1	2	2	0	3,471	20th	$2,683,225
2002	36	0	2	7	0	3,418	23rd	$3,390,690
2003	36	0	2	9	2	3,525	22nd	$3,660,174
Totals	177	1	4	20	2	16,495		$12,946,992

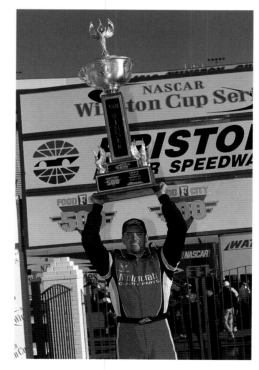

Opposite Page: Elliott Sadler, driver of the No. 38 Robert Yates Racing Ford, seems to portray an intense stare, as do the characters embroidered onto his uniform. Top Left: Sadler is dressed and ready for the command to fire his engine. It is a ritual he had enjoyed since joining the NASCAR Winston Cup circuit in 1999. Top Right: Sadler's colorful machine is easily noticed at any point on the race track, no matter where he races. Right: Sadler excelled to a new level with his first career victory at Bristol Motor Speedway in March 2001. Below: Driving for Wood Brothers Racing, Sadler puts his No. 21 Ford to the test at Darlington Raceway in March 2001.

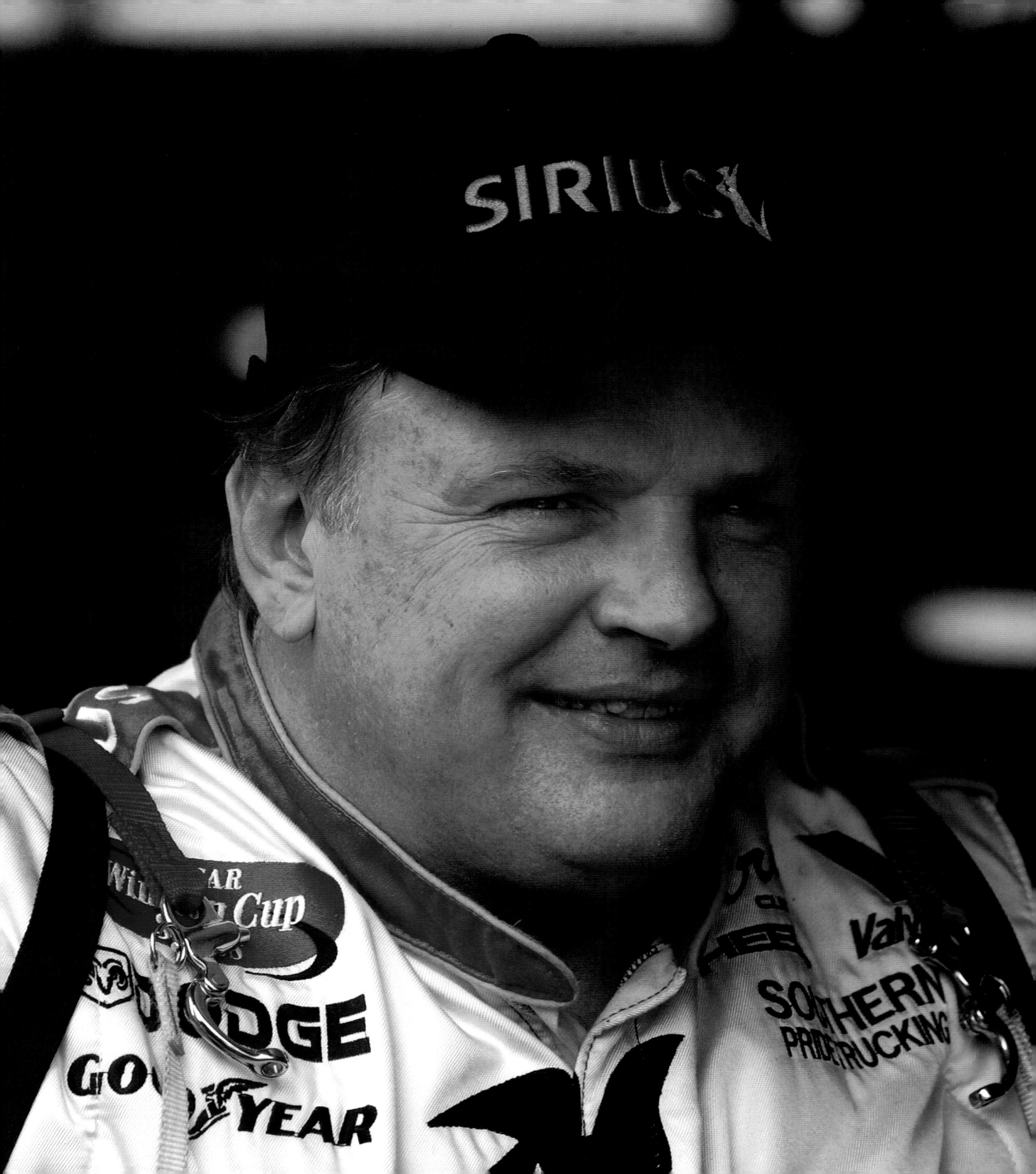
Cup
YEAR
PRIDETRUCKING

JIMMY SPENCER

Born:
February 15, 1957
Berwick, Pennsylvania

Height: 6-0

Weight: 230 lbs

7

Sponsor
Sirius Satellite
Make
Dodge
Crew Chief

Ever Ever since Jimmy Spencer arrived on the NASCAR Winston Cup scene, he has been known to stir things up, especially when a long and uneventful race really needs stirring. He's been benched by NASCAR officials and even fined, but he's still just as outspoken as ever. The native of Berwick, Pennsylvania, knows nothing but pushing the throttle to the floor and cranking the wheel hard left.

In 1986 and 1987, Spencer showed he was serious about winning when he collected back-to-back Winston modified championships. He progressed the next season into the NASCAR Busch Series, and he continues to compete in that series along with his Winston Cup efforts. In his first Winston Cup experience, Spencer ran 17 races in 1989 for legend-turned-owner Buddy Baker. There, too, Spencer showed great promise but just couldn't break into the winner's circle. Team owners Rod Osterland and Travis Carter also enjoyed good finishes with Spencer in 1990 and 1991, respectively.

Because of Spencer's strong efforts in the series, another legendary former driver, Bobby Allison, invited him to join his team for the Winston Cup Series in 1992. Over a two-year period, Spencer had 13 top-10 finishes in Allison's Fords, including a high of second place at the Winston 500 at Talladega in 1993.

NASCAR Winston Cup Career Statistics

Year	Races	Wins	Top 5s	Top 10s	Poles	Total Points	Final Standing	Winnings
1989	17	0	0	3	0	1,570	34th	$121,065
1990	26	0	0	2	0	2,579	24th	$219,775
1991	29	0	1	6	0	2,790	25th	$283,620
1992	12	0	3	3	0	1,284	33rd	$186,085
1993	30	0	5	10	0	3,496	12th	$686,026
1994	29	2	3	4	1	2,613	29th	$479,235
1995	29	0	0	4	0	2,809	26th	$507,210
1996	31	0	2	9	0	3,476	15th	$1,090,876
1997	32	0	1	4	0	3,079	20th	$1,073,779
1998	31	0	3	8	0	3,464	14th	$1,741,012
1999	34	0	2	4	0	3,312	20th	$1,752,299
2000	34	0	2	5	0	3,188	22nd	$1,936,762
2001	36	0	3	8	2	3,782	16th	$2,669,638
2002	34	0	2	6	0	3,187	27th	$2,136,790
2003	35	0	1	4	0	3,147	29th	$2,565,803
Totals	439	2	28	80	3	43,776		$17,449,975

Opposite Page: Jimmy Spencer, driver of the Ultra Motorsports Dodge, is known as someone with a rather colorful personality often in the headlines. The Pennsylvania native has two-career NASCAR Winston Cup victories to his credit. Right: Spencer takes his No.7 Dodge through its paces at speed during one of many laps turned during the 2003 season.

Above: Spencer's crew works to change his tires and add fuel during a routine pit stop. Right: Spencer looks to be studying the happenings in the garage area in this July 1999 photograph at Pocono Raceway, a facility he calls his home track.

Then came Junior Johnson, a man known for winning races and championships. Johnson's desire for drivers to push the button, and the fact that Spencer knew no other way to race, made for a perfect pair. At the start of the 1994 Winston Cup season, Spencer immediately showed his strength at the Daytona 500, and then went on to win the Pepsi 400 there in July and the DieHard 500 at Talladega three weeks later, notching victories at the two foremost restrictor-plate tracks.

Spencer elected to return to the cars fielded by Travis Carter in 1995, but found little success. Still, the driver and team owner remained together until the end of the 2001 season.

For 2002 Spencer hooked up with Chip Ganassi and Felix Sabates, driving Dodges for the first time in his career. Spencer could only muster two top-five and six top-10s and was released from the team at the end of the season. From there, Spencer elected to join Jim Smith in 2003 and enjoyed some strong runs. Still, the final statistics didn't reflect the team's true potential.

"There have been times when we've really shown some promise in 2003 and on the other side of that, we've had our share of problems," Spencer says. "I'm certain about one thing; this is a tough race team that can win races. We're not there yet but there's still time to win one."

TONY STEWART

20

Born:
May 20, 1971
Rushville, Indiana

Height: 5-9

Weight: 170 lbs

Sponsor	
Home Depot	
Make	
Pontiac	
Crew Chief	

When Tony Stewart arrived in the NASCAR Winston Cup arena to drive Pontiacs for team owner Joe Gibbs, most everyone billed him as a likely instant winner. The Indiana native had already spent many years winning races in the Open Wheel Sprint Car ranks as well as in the most elite of open-wheel arenas, the Indianapolis 500. With such tremendous talent established so early on, the gates of Victory Lane would most certainly not be padlocked long while he was around.

Stewart exceeded expectations and began his Winston Cup portfolio by breaking the record for wins by a rookie and winning the 1999 NASCAR Winston Cup Rookie of the Year. His first career victory came in his 25th start, at Richmond International Raceway in Virginia. By season's end, Stewart and his team were clicking well enough to win back-to-back races at Phoenix, Arizona, and Homestead, Florida.

Perhaps Stewart's most impressive accomplishment of 1999 was racing in both the Coca-Cola World 600 at Charlotte and the Indianapolis 500 on the same day.

NASCAR Winston Cup Career Statistics

Year	Races	Wins	Top 5s	Top 10s	Poles	Total Points	Final Standing	Winnings
1999	34	3	12	21	2	4,774	4th	$3,190,149
2000	34	6	12	23	2	4,570	6th	$3,642,348
2001	36	3	15	22	0	4,763	2nd	$4,941,463
2002	36	3	15	21	4	4,800	1st	$4,695,150
2003	36	2	12	18	1	4,549	7th	$5,227,503
Totals	176	17	66	105	9	23,456		$21,696,613

Above: Tony Stewart is set and ready for action as he awaits the start of the race at Rockingham in October 2000.

Left: Stewart's orange-and-white Pontiac is one of the most recognized rides on the Winston Cup circuit, especially after the championship run in 2002.

Above: Stewart shares a laugh with Joe Gibbs Racing teammate Bobby Labonte in the garage area at Darlington in 2000. Left: Stewart shows his anger toward Kenny Irwin after the two made contact on the track at Martinsville, Virginia, in March 1999.

After an exhaustive 1,100 miles of high-speed magic, he finished fourth in the 600 at Charlotte Motor Speedway and ninth in the 500 at Indianapolis Motor Speedway.

In 2000, many looked to Stewart to pull off the rare accomplishment of winning a Winston Cup championship the very next year after capturing rookie honors. Unfortunately, Stewart got off to a slow start in his sophomore season, ultimately finishing a respectable sixth in points, while teammate Bobby Labonte captured his first Winston Cup championship.

The next year, Tony Stewart enjoyed his best season to date. He started 2001 off with a victory in the Bud Shoot-Out, a special non-points event for pole-position winners. In June, he was a winner on the road course at Sears Point, California. He followed that performance with another victory at Richmond and also pulled off a win at the demanding high-banked short track of Bristol Motor Speedway. In the end, he finished second to Jeff Gordon in the overall championship hunt after coming on strong at the end when others suffered mechanical failures.

For the second time in his career, Stewart attempted the Charlotte-Indy double duty in 2001. He again finished strong, coming in sixth in the 500 and third in the 600 at Charlotte. He elected not to do so in 2002, knowing the championship race needed his full attention.

That year, Stewart was successful and

put together his first-career NASCAR Winston Cup championship with three victories, 15 top-fives and 21 top-10s in 36 starts.

For 2003, Stewart enjoyed a win at Pocono, Pennsylvania and several races where he challenged for the win but settled for top-five finishes.

"When you have a year like we did last year, we needed a lot of luck at the end of the year to help us get to where we were, and that's what happened," Stewart says. "We had some good luck happen to us.

"We went from everything being really good at the end of (2002) to things starting off good, then going South on us. Now, hopefully, it's coming back to the other side of that circle and coming full circle."

Top: Stewart leads the field at Lowe's Motor Speedway in October 2000. Even though he has yet to win at the 1.5-mile speedway, some of his best finishes have come at the Charlotte track. Above: Number 1! Stewart's victory in the MBNA America 500 at Atlanta Motor Speedway helped him down the road to a championship in 2002. Left: Stewart makes a pit stop at Las Vegas in March 2002 en route to recording another top-5 finish.

KENNY WALLACE

23

Born:
August 23, 1963
St. Louis, Missouri

Height: 5-11

Weight: 180 lbs

Sponsor
Stacker2
Make
Dodge

enny Wallace may still be looking for that elusive first victory on the NASCAR Winston Cup circuit, but the laughs come easy for this would-be stand-up comic. While filling in as an interim driver for Dale Earnhardt Inc. in Steve Park's Chevrolets, Wallace has nothing but jokes to tell in the garage areas on the 36-race schedule. But when it comes to standing on the throttle in any of the Winston Cup or Busch Series cars he drives, it's no laughing matter.

The native of Fenton, Missouri, and younger brother of 1989 Winston Cup champion Rusty Wallace has proven that he can take a racecar to the front of the field on a Sunday afternoon. In 2002, he split his time between the top two series while Park recuperated from head injuries suffered during a Busch Series event at Darlington Raceway in September 2001.

For 11 seasons, Wallace has shown some impressive moves on the racetrack. Known as "Herman" in the garage area for the name he uses on the two-way radio during races, Wallace is always creating a stir with his hardy laugh and infectious grin.

Wallace feels good about the upcoming 2004 NASCAR season, even though this past season offered some disappointments.

"At the end of 2002, we were qualifying well and I thought we were making some pretty strong gains," Wallace says. "The 2003 season was definitely a disappointment. But it's not for the lack of effort. The 2003 season has been like the Richard Petty commercial where he says, 'You can't get upset over one bad race or one bad year.' Nothing devastating has gone bad. It's just that it hasn't been the year we were hoping for."

NASCAR Winston Cup Career Statistics

Year	Races	Wins	Top 5s	Top 10s	Poles	Total Points	Final Standing	Winnings
1990	1	0	0	0	0	85	--	$96,050
1991	5	0	0	0	0	412	44th	$58,325
1993	30	0	0	3	0	2,893	23rd	$330,325
1994	12	0	1	3	0	1,413	40th	$235,005
1995	11	0	0	0	0	875	42nd	$151,700
1996	30	0	0	2	0	2,694	28th	$457,665
1997	31	0	0	2	2	2,462	33rd	$939,001
1998	31	0	0	7	0	2,615	31st	$1,019,861
1999	34	0	3	5	0	3,210	22nd	$1,416,208
2000	34	0	1	1	0	2,877	26th	$1,723,966
2001	24	0	1	2	1	2,054	39th	$1,507,922
2002	21	0	0	1	0	1,868	39th	$1,379,800
2003	36	0	0	1	0	3,061	30th	$2,480,492
Totals	300	0	6	27	3	26,520		$11,796,320

Above: Kenny Wallace motors around the bend in his dodge. Left: Wallace waits in anticipation for the start of the race.

RUSTY WALLACE

Born:
August 14, 1956
Fenton, Missouri

Height: 6-0

Weight: 185 lbs

2

Sponsor
Miller Lite
Make
Dodge
Crew Chief

There are few drivers in any type of auto racing who have enjoyed the fan following Rusty Wallace has enjoyed. On top of his game or struggling for position, his fans are loyal, sticking by him in the best or worst of streaks.

When a bushy-haired Rusty Wallace brought a Roger Penske–owned Chevrolet to Atlanta Motor Speedway on March 16, 1980, the young Missourian wasn't supposed to have much of a chance. After all, he was a rookie competing in his first Winston Cup event. But Wallace made the most of his ride that day, mixing it up with the veterans of the sport and making it look easy. Wallace was leading with 29 laps to go when Dale Earnhardt passed him for the win. Wallace held on for second place, and the sensational debut was an indication of things to come.

Wallace won rookie honors in USAC competition in 1979 and was the 1983 ASA champion. Wallace established himself throughout the Midwest as a strong threat to win anywhere he raced, and he entered select Cup races, hungry for a ride in the big show. In his first full season in NASCAR Winston Cup racing, Wallace teamed with owner Cliff Stewart to become the 1984 Rookie of the Year. His first victory came in the 76th start of his career, on April 6, 1986, at Bristol Motor Speedway.

Within just two years Wallace was contending for the championship, finishing as

NASCAR Winston Cup Career Statistics

Year	Races	Wins	Top 5s	Top 10s	Poles	Total Points	Final Standing	Winnings
1980	2	0	1	1	0	291	--	$22,760
1981	4	0	0	1	0	399	--	$12,895
1982	3	0	0	0	0	186	--	$7,655
1983	0	0	0	0	0	0	--	$1,100
1984	30	0	2	4	0	3,316	14th	$195,927
1985	28	0	2	8	0	2,867	19th	$233,670
1986	29	2	4	16	0	3,757	6th	$557,354
1987	29	2	9	16	1	3,818	5th	$690,652
1988	29	6	19	23	2	4,464	2nd	$1,411,567
1989	29	6	13	20	4	4,176	1st	$2,247,950
1990	29	2	9	16	2	3,676	6th	$954,129
1991	29	2	9	14	2	3,582	10th	$502,073
1992	29	1	5	12	1	3,556	13th	$657,925
1993	30	10	19	21	3	4,446	2nd	$1,702,154
1994	31	8	17	20	2	4,207	3rd	$1,914,072
1995	31	2	15	19	0	4,240	5th	$1,642,837
1996	31	5	8	18	0	3,717	7th	$1,665,315
1997	32	1	8	12	1	3,598	9th	$1,705,625
1998	33	1	15	21	4	4,501	4th	$2,667,889
1999	34	1	7	16	4	4,155	8th	$2,454,050
2000	34	4	12	20	9	4,544	7th	$3,621,468
2001	36	1	8	14	0	4,481	7th	$4,788,652
2002	36	0	7	17	1	4,574	7th	$4,090,050
2003	36	0	2	12	0	3,950	14th	$3,766,744
Totals	634	54	191	321	36	80,501		$37,514,510

Always a threat to win in his Penske Racing Ford, Rusty Wallace shows his muscle at Bristol in March 2002. It was one of several top-10 finishes for the Miller Lite car.

runner-up for the 1988 Winston Cup title to Bill Elliott by only 24 points. A year later, after a season-long battle with Earnhardt, Wallace was crowned the 1989 NASCAR Winston Cup champion with team owner Raymond Beadle, inching out The Intimidator by 12 points.

After an 11-year separation, Wallace joined up again with Roger Penske in 1991, now as an established winner. His best years in the victory category came in 1993 and 1994, when he logged 18 wins in 61 starts over the two seasons. At the end of the 1996 season, Wallace won the inaugural Suzuka Thunder 100, a special non-points event held in Suzuka, Japan.

Wallace is undoubtedly one of the hottest stars in Winston Cup racing, having won at least one race in every season since

1986. He constantly demands more and more perfection from his crew. With Roger Penske, a longtime motorsports magnate who has enjoyed much success in Indy car racing, Wallace knows the chemistry is always there for success. Over a 17-year period, Wallace has collected 54 Winston Cup victories, 36 of them with Penske's organization. Now, all Wallace wants is more wins and at least one more Winston Cup championship before he someday turns his attention to other business ventures.

"We've had a few races slip away over the years for one reason or another," Wallace says. "But I know I've got 54 wins in record books and a championship in 1989 that I'm proud of. I'd like to get a few more wins and another championship before I stop driving."

Top Left: Wallace enjoys the cheers he receives at Bristol Motor Speedway in August 1998. He often admits that Bristol is one of his favorite tracks. Top Right: Wallace speeds along the concrete at Rockingham early in the 2002 season. Right: Wallace is in a familiar pose behind the controls of the Penske Racing Ford at New Hampshire in 1997.

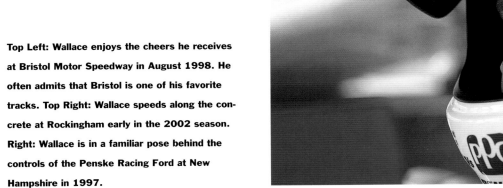

Above: Wallace makes a pit stop at Sears Point Raceway in California, a track where he earned victories in 1990 and again in 1996. Left: Wallace enjoys a spare moment in the garage area at Dover in June 2001. The 1989 Winston Cup Champion would love to have another taste of the title before he retires. Right: Wallace raises his arms in victory after taking the checkered flag at Bristol Motor Speedway in March 2000. It was Wallace's 53rd career win.

MICHAEL WALTRIP

15

Born:
April 30, 1963
Owensboro, Kentucky

Height: 6-5

Weight: 210 lbs

Sponsor
NAPA
Make
Chevrolet

Michael Waltrip is quick to tell you that stock cars aren't his only racing passion. The Owensboro, Kentucky, native has entered both the Boston Marathon and the Tampa Marathon. But it's in the NASCAR arena where his greatest talents lie, and like his teammate Kenny Wallace, Waltrip certainly knows how to hold court in any garage area.

The younger brother of three-time Winston Cup champion Darrell Waltrip, Michael is probably best known for his victory in the 2001 Daytona 500, in the 462nd start of a career dating back to 1985. The victory will forever be overshadowed by the death of Dale Earnhardt on the final lap—ironically, Waltrip was driving a Chevrolet owned by Earnhardt. He was in the lead, two positions ahead of the legend when the fatal crash occurred.

Waltrip returned to Daytona in July of that year and finished second to DEI teammate Dale Earnhardt Jr. in the 400-mile event. Waltrip now has over 500 starts in a career that also includes 21 top fives, 85 top 10s, and 2 pole positions. Waltrip captured a second career victory in 2002, and once again the trophy was earned at the famous Daytona International Speedway. The win in the Pepsi 400 that July supplied Waltrip brought encouragement for continued success with DEI.

In 2003, Waltrip scored his second career Daytona 500 in a rain-shortened event. He followed that win by taking the checkered flag at Talladega Superspeedway in October to help the DEI cars dominate those two tracks.

""Remember this: Dale Earnhardt was the best at Daytona and Talladega, and he knew that to be the best, you had to have the best cars," Waltrip says. "When he

NASCAR Winston Cup Career Statistics

Year	Races	Wins	Top 5s	Top 10s	Poles	Total Points	Final Standing	Winnings
1985	5	0	0	0	0	395	49th	$9,540
1986	28	0	0	0	0	2,853	19th	$108,767
1987	29	0	0	1	0	2,840	20th	$205,370
1988	29	0	1	3	0	2,949	18th	$240,400
1989	29	0	0	5	0	3,067	18th	$249,233
1990	29	0	5	10	0	3,251	16th	$395,507
1991	29	0	4	12	2	3,254	15th	$440,812
1992	29	0	1	2	0	2,825	23rd	$410,545
1993	30	0	0	5	0	3,291	17th	$529,923
1994	31	0	2	10	0	3,512	12th	$706,426
1995	31	0	2	8	0	3,601	12th	$898,338
1996	31	0	1	11	0	3,535	14th	$1,182,811
1997	32	0	0	6	0	3,173	18th	$1,138,599
1998	32	0	0	5	0	3,340	17th	$1,508,680
1999	34	0	1	3	0	2,974	29th	$1,701,160
2000	34	0	1	1	0	2,792	27th	$1,689,421
2001	36	1	3	3	0	3,159	24th	$3,411,644
2002	36	1	4	10	0	3,985	14th	$2,829,180
2003	36	2	8	11	0	3,934	15th	$4,463,485
Totals	570	4	33	106	2	58,764		$22,119,841

Michael Waltrip pushes his Dale Earnhardt Inc. Chevrolet to top speed around Richmond International Speedway in Virginia in May 2002.

started DEI, he made sure that everyone understood that he would have the best restrictor-plate cars. He was going to have cars that were faster than everyone else's, to give the drivers a chance to win. That was his signature at DEI. We're going to do whatever it takes to have the best program. He left his fingerprints all over DEI when he left us, and we just understand that it is our job to continue to execute and perform and build the type of equipment that he would be proud of. Dale is gone, but he is such a presence at our shop, and a presence when it comes to plate racing."

INDEX

24 Hours of Daytona, 49
Allison, Bobby, 23, 24, 39, 77, 111
Allison, Davey, 55, 82
American Race Car Association, 73, 97, 101
American Speed Association, 9, 77
Andretti, John, 82
ARTGO Series, 63
Ascot Speedway (CA), 13
Atlanta Motor Speedway (GA), 17, 27, 40, 46, 53, 75, 89, 97, 117, 121
Atwood, Casey, 75
Automobile Racing Club of America, 82, 93
Baja 1000, 49
Baker, Buddy, 105, 111
Baldwin, Tommy, 24, 25
Barbour, Scott, 33
Beadle, Raymond, 122
Benson, Johnny, 8, 9
Bernstein, Kenny, 17, 106
Beverly, Tim, 9
Biffle, Greg, 10, 11
Bill Davis Racing, 24, 25, 67
Blaney, Dave, 12–15
Bodine, Brett, 16, 17
Bodine, Geoff, 77
Bonnett, Neil, 55
Borland, Matt, 94
Bowers, Nelson, 9, 33
Brickyard 400, 39, 46, 47, 53, 56, 57, 67
Bristol Motor Speedway (TN), 28, 29, 109, 117, 121–123
Brooklyn, Michigan, 56
Buck Baker Driving School, 45
Bud Shoot-Out, 117
Budweiser 400, 106
Burton, Jeff, 19–21, 23, 24
Burton, Ward, 22–25
Busch Clash, 46
Busch, Kurt, 26–29, 31
California Speedway, 28, 43, 60, 82, 95
Caraway Speedway, 66
Carter, Travis, 111, 113
Champion, Bill, 105
Charlotte Motor Speedway (NC), 21, 24, 36, 40, 46, 56, 59, 61, 63, 79, 83, 85, 93, 94, 98, 105, 117
Chicagoland Speedway, 53, 60
Childress, Richard, 51, 53, 98, 106
Coca-Cola 600, 24, 46, 56, 63, 102, 115
Craftsman Truck Series, 11, 27, 53, 91
Craven, Ricky, 30–33

Cunningham, H. B., 73
Dale Earnhardt Inc., 36, 97, 119, 125
Darlington Raceway, 21, 24, 31, 33, 40, 45, 55, 56, 69, 70, 71, 73, 74, 77, 82, 93, 98, 99, 101, 103, 109, 119
Davis, Bill, 15, 24, 45
Daytona 500, 9, 28, 40, 53, 56, 57, 69, 74, 79, 98, 113, 125
Daytona Beach, 99
Daytona International Speedway, 11, 35, 37, 46, 56, 59, 65, 73, 82, 101, 103 125
DEI, 99
DieHard 500, 113
Digard Racing, 106
Dilliard, A. G., 24
Donlavey, Junie, 51, 105
Dover Downs International Speedway (DE), 20, 29, 37, 60, 69, 81, 82, 97, 98, 106, 123
Earnhardt Jr., Dale, 34–37, 125
Earnhardt Sr., Dale, 25, 46, 51, 53, 56, 70, 97, 105 121, 122, 125
Earnhardt, Kerry, 36
Ellington, Hoss, 17
Elliot, Bill, 38–41, 89, 122
Elliot, Ernie, 74
Evernham Motorsports, 81–83
Evernham, Ray, 39, 41
Featherlite Southwest Tour, 27
Fennig, Jimmy, 28
First Union 400, 17
Fittapaldi, Christian, 42, 43
Fittapaldi, Emerson, 43
Fontana, California, 60, 99
Foyt, A. J., 49
Foyt, Larry, 98
Ganassi Racing, 85, 87
Ganassi, Chip, 74, 85, 113
Gibbs, Joe, 56, 65, 115, 116
Gordon, Jeff, 13, 44–47, 53, 56, 59, 60, 67, 69, 93, 94, 117
Gordon, Robby, 48–51
Grand Prix of Houston, 87
Green Brothers, 81
Gunderman, J., 78
Haas, Carl, 43
Haas, Gene, 25
Hagan, Billy, 65, 69, 74
Hamby, Roger, 74, 78
Hampton Georgia, 28
Hardy, Charles, 41
Harvick, Kevin, 52, 53
Hedrick, Larry, 31
Hendrick Motorsports, 31, 46, 59, 60, 69, 70, 89, 93, 94
Hendrick, Rick, 17, 31, 59, 60, 89, 106

Hickory Motor Speedway (NC), 55
Hicks, Hal, 33
Homestead International Speedway (FL), 28, 29, 39, 67, 115
IMSA road race series, 49
Indianapolis 500, 39, 43, 46, 47, 51, 53, 56, 57, 61, 115, 117
Irvan, Ernie, 56
Irwin, Kenny, 116
Jackson, Richard, 70, 89
Jarrett, Dale, 54–57, 67, 94
Jarrett, Ned, 55
Joe Gibbs Racing, 67
Johnson, Jimmie, 58–61, 94
Johnson, Junior, 17, 70, 113
Kansas Speedway, 56, 82, 93, 94
Kenseth, Matt, 17, 36, 62, 63
Kentucky Motor Speedway, 81, 93
Knaus, Chad, 60, 61
Knoxville Nationals, 13
Kranefuss, Michael, 82
Labonte, Bobby, 64–67, 85, 98, 116, 117
Labonte, Terry, 46, 56, 65, 66, 68–71
Las Vegas Motor Speedway, 9, 19, 21, 23, 63, 65, 74, 79, 83, 117
Leslie, Ben, 28
Lowe's Motor Speedway (NC), 17, 59, 63, 85, 117
Marine, Mark, 28
Marlin, Clifton "Coo Coo," 73
Marlin, Sterling, 72–75, 85, 87
Martin, Mark, 63, 76–79
Martinsville Speedway (VA), 20, 25, 28, 32, 33, 74, 85, 97, 107, 113, 116
Martocci, Filbert, 19
Masa Marin, 87
Mast, Rick, 24
May, Dick, 69
Mayfield, Jeremy, 80–83
MB2 Motorsports, 89
MBV Motorsports, 9
McMurray, Jamie, 84, 85, 87
McSwaim, Michael "Fatback," 65
Mears, Casey, 86, 87
Mears, Rick, 87
Melling, Harry, 39
Michigan International Speedway, 28, 56, 63, 73, 75, 94, 97, 113
Miller 400, 56
Miller, Don, 93
Moore, Bud, 17, 106
Moran-McClure Racing, 74

Moroso, Dick, 31
Nadeau, Jerry, 88, 89, 91
NAPA Auto Parts 500, 95
Nashville Speedway (TN), 73, 74
National 500, 105
National Motorsports Press Association, 41
Nemechek, Joe, 11, 90, 91
Nemechek, John, 91
New England 300, 24
New Hampshire International Speedway, 19–21, 24, 25, 31, 39, 51, 83, 91, 94, 95, 102, 103, 122
Newman, Paul, 43
Newman, Ryan, 60, 92–95
North Carolina Motor Speedway, 9, 21, 31, 39, 41, 56, 63, 78, 82, 98, 107, 115, 122
North Wilkesboro, 17, 70
Osterland, Rod, 111
Pacific Coast Nationals, 13
Panch, Marcin, 109
Parhump Valley Speedway, 27
Park, Bob, 97
Park, Steve, 96–99, 119
Parrott, Todd, 56
Pearson, David, 70, 109
Pearson, Larry, 17
Penske Racing, 82, 83, 93, 122
Penske, Roger, 82, 121, 122
Pepsi 400, 11, 113, 125
Petree, Andy, 11
Petty Enterprises, 43, 89, 102
Petty, Kyle, 11, 43, 100–103
Petty, Lee, 102
Petty, Richard, 43, 45, 102, 109
Phoenix International Raceway (AZ), 19, 21, 32, 43, 59, 63, 115
Pocono International Speedway (PA), 25, 39, 43, 55-57, 66, 71, 82, 93, 112, 117
PPI Motorsports, 31
Putnam, Gary, 43
RCR Enterprises, 35, 50, 53
Rexford, 46
Reynolds, R. J., 40
Richmond International Speedway (VA), 35, 63, 66, 83, 89, 102, 115, 117, 125
Rider, Chuck, 9
Riverside, California, 40, 106
Road America, 43
Robert Yates Racing, 55, 107, 109
Roger Penske, 93, 94
Roush Racing, 11, 19, 20, 27, 49, 69
Roush, Jack, 9, 11, 27, 28, 49, 63, 78

Rudd Sr., Al, 105
Rudd, Ricky, 70, 104–107
Sabates, Felix, 102, 113
Sadler, Earl, 82
Sadler, Elliot, 108, 109
Sauter, Jim, 77
SCORE Off-Road Trophy Truck Championship, 51
Sears Point Raceway (CA), 117, 123
Sharon Speedway, 15
Sharp, Scott, 33
Shepherd, Morgan, 11
Smith, John, 113
Sonoma, California, 27, 51
Sospenzo, Peter, 91
South Boston Speedway (VA), 19, 24
Southern 500, 24, 40, 69, 70, 71
Spencer, Jimmy, 110–113
Sprint Car, 15, 93
Stacy, J. D., 77
Stadium Series, 49
Stavola Brothers Racing, 74
Stavola, Bill, 21
Stavola, Mickey, 21
Stewart, Cliff, 121
Stewart, Jackie, 45
Stewart, Tony, 28, 114–117
Suzuka Thunder 100, 122
Talladega Superspeedway (GA), 33, 37, 40, 67, 73, 74, 82, 85, 109, 111, 109
Taylor, T. W., 82
Texas Motor Speedway, 36, 63, 71, 73, 82, 103
Thompson, Mickey, 49
Trickle, Dick, 77
Turner, Chris, 109
Ulrich, D. K., 78
Ultra Motorsports, 111
Vickers, Brian, 91
Wallace, Kenny, 118, 119
Wallace, Rusty, 46, 69, 93, 120–123
Waltrip, Darrell, 106, 125
Waltrip, Michael, 124, 125
Warren, Frank, 70
Watkins Glen International (NY), 49–51, 97, 99
Wells, Cal, 31, 33
Winston 500, 111
Wood Brothers Racing, 109
Wood Brothers, 55, 56, 102, 107
World of Outlaws, 13, 15
World Sprint Car championship, 13
Yarborough, Cale, 55, 82, 105
Yates, Robert, 51, 56, 67, 106
Zervackis, Emmanuel, 55

128